dramatic
Encounters
with God

Nicole Johnson

Published by
THOMAS NELSON™
Since 1798

www.thomasnelson.com

© 2007 Nicole Johnson

Published in Nashville, Tennessee by Thomas Nelson, Inc.

Agent: Mel Berger

All Scripture quotations, unless otherwise indicated, are taken from the New
King James Version. Copyright © 1982 by Thomas Nelson, Inc. Used by
permission. All rights reserved.

Library of Congress Cataloging-in-Publication Data

Johnson, Nicole, 1966–
  Dramatic encounters with God / by Nicole Johnson.
    p. cm.
  ISBN-13: 978-0-8499-0357-1 (hardcover)
  ISBN-10: 0-8499-0357-2 (hardcover)
  1. Meditations. 2. Jesus Christ—Meditations. 3. Bible. N.T. Gospels—
Meditations. 4. Love—Religious aspects—Christianity—Meditations. I. Title.
  BV4832.3.J65 2007
  242'.5—dc22   2006038714

Printed in the United States of America
07 08 09 10 11 QW 5 4 3 2 1

Also by
Nicole Johnson

Contents

Introduction

*I*t was just a voice on a hot dusty road, asking a straight-forward question, "Saul, why are you persecuting me?" . . . and a dramatic encounter with God changed the course of the world. From Adam in the Garden of Eden to Moses on Mt. Sinai to Saul on the road to Damascus, God has a history of interrupting our so-called everyday lives with his presence (and on rare occasions, with his voice). When he does, it's a dramatic encounter like no other. Something happens that stops us in our tracks—it at once exposes us and embraces us. Something happens that reveals God in a new way and brings him near. Something happens that changes our direction or our perspective or our soul, and then the rest of our lives. It can happen anywhere. On a busy street, on a business trip overseas, or right in the middle of our morning coffee—whenever God grasps our human hearts and allows us to hear his voice, it is a dramatic encounter.

What would it have been like to be there in the first century when Christ was interacting with people directly? In the days when the holy met the human face-to-face, when God walked among the people, captivating them with his message of love? It is hard to imagine all the encounters that took place in almost every footprint he made. Yet it is worth trying because of what we learn in the process. People matter so much more to God than we think and thus believe. It is easy and understandable to read first-century encounters with Jesus as just stories about other people—blind people, lame children, or religious leaders—who lived in another place and time. But when we take a closer look, we find that they are about us, here and now, and they are about love.

The Power of Love

Love is far and away the strongest power known to humankind. The power of love could eradicate the need for weapons of mass destruction. The power of love could change all that our prison system was designed to correct. So why doesn't it? Sadly, love is an undervalued, often untapped resource. People underestimate its strength. But love reveals its power when we realize it can do something that nothing else on the face of the earth can do: love can change the human heart.

You don't need money
Don't take fame
Don't need no credit card to ride this train
It's strong and it's sudden and it's cruel sometimes
But it might just save your life . . .
That's the power of love

Huey Lewis might not have set out to write a gospel song, but he did just that. His lyrics captured an old truth in a new way when "The Power of Love" was recorded in 1985. That same year, the producers of a film called *Back to the Future* chose Lewis' lyrics to underscore the film's message: love has the power to change things even across time and space, which is why sometimes you have to revisit the past in order to change your future.

That's what this book is all about. We revisit the past—the Jerusalem of the ancient world where Christ walked as a man—so that his love can change our twenty-first-century futures. We meet him on that dusty road, or on the steps of the temple, or in the house of his friends, to listen in on his divine conversation.

And as we watch his interactions and experience his love, our daily lives of car pools and time clocks and dishes and budgets are changed forever.

By going back, we can discover for ourselves that divine love is strong enough to break destructive patterns. As God speaks to us from his Word, our hearts are transformed, our eyes are opened, our feet learn to walk in new paths, and our religion becomes a relationship.

If you've ever doubted your faith, if you've ever done something wrong and desperately needed grace, if you've been betrayed by someone you loved, if you've struggled with issues of control, come walk by the Sea of Galilee, stand with Christ in the Garden of Gethsemane, gather in the stony circle around the adulterous woman, and see what happens in your own heart.

On our own, we do not have the ability to love like God does. But when we tap into his love, it makes our small amount of love more abundant and free. It transforms our little love into the kind of big love that can forgive betrayal—or lay down our blades of cutting, or smooth the wrinkles of our doubt—the kind of love that can change our lives. Really experiencing this book will require a good deal of honesty and courage.

Can you look for yourself in every story—and admit when

you find you? Rarely do we take the time to answer the kinds of questions that are included at the end of each chapter in this book. They provide an opportunity for a private self-inventory—one that can lead toward growth and change. We can make internal decisions about who we want to be . . . but never as strongly as when we are honest with ourselves about who we are. Only then can we know in what direction we have to go to reflect the loving father who created us. So take a deep breath, ask God to interrupt your life today with his divine presence, and hold your heart still as you dive into your own dramatic encounter with him.

Chapter 1

Are You the One?

A dramatic encounter for John the Baptist

Life-Changing Lesson:
Love can handle doubt

Biblical Passage:
Luke 7:18–23
(Optional parallel passage: Matthew 11:2–11)

Then the disciples of John reported to him concerning all these things. And John, calling two of his disciples to him, sent them to Jesus, saying, "Are You the Coming One, or do we look for another?"

When the men had come to Him, they said, "John the Baptist has sent us to You, saying, 'Are You the Coming One, or do we look for another?'" And that very hour He cured many of infirmities, afflictions, and evil spirits; and to many blind He gave sight.

Jesus answered and said to them, "Go and tell John the things you have seen and heard: that the blind see, the lame walk, the lepers are cleansed, the deaf hear, the dead are raised, the poor have the gospel preached to them. And blessed is he who is not offended because of Me." (Luke 7:18–23)

*J*ohn was in prison. All he knew about what Jesus was doing came from hearing the reports of others. And what they were reporting was that there was a prophet in Judea, the likes of whom none had ever seen before. John ached and yearned to see it with his own eyes; it was what he had lived his whole life for. He thought back to the day when Jesus came to the river Jordan to find John the Baptist and asked to be baptized. This was a day unlike any other in his life. His belief that God had finally sent the Messiah was like a fire in his soul, and he preached and baptized amid the flames of his heart.

But now those flames had become dying embers and doubts were forming in his mind. He listened carefully to the reports of his own disciples, men he trusted, but now they were gone, John was full of questions. *Is Jesus really the One?* While he couldn't believe he was thinking such thoughts, he found himself powerless not to think them.

Maybe it didn't even matter if Jesus was the One. Either way, John thought he would probably be killed. He had spoken out against the horrific wrong of a very powerful ruler, Herod, and he was in prison because of it. John's greatest gift was not diplomacy. He was passionate about the kingdom of God—and in the kingdom, men of God don't sit idly by while a powerful ruler commits adultery. Herod had taken his half brother's wife, Herodias, to be his own. John was a preacher of repentance and not afraid to name names. He proclaimed that what Herod and Herodias had done was not only wrong, but wicked, and they must repent because the kingdom of God was at hand. Herod and Herodias decided they would like it a lot better if John weren't roaming the countryside influencing public opinion.

But now, in his cell, John wondered if the kingdom was as close as he had once believed. He wanted to talk to Jesus, but he couldn't. He was alone, with only his thoughts, and seeds of doubt were growing in his mind.

It was dark in John's cell. The air was thick and hot as he wrestled with feverish questions. What if Jesus wasn't who he'd thought he was? Was it even possible that he could be the promised Messiah, the long-awaited deliverer of the people? His hope ran so deep, but his doubts did too.

Have I wanted it to be true so much that I was seeing something that wasn't there? Did Jesus ever come right out and say it? Does he even think he is the Messiah? What good is my thinking he's the Messiah if he doesn't even think he's the Messiah? And deeper still, *Should the Messiah know he's the Messiah, or will he just be the Messiah and we'll know?*

John was having a crisis of faith.

The series of events that brings on such doubt is different for each of us. We don't have to be in prison to start asking the deepest questions of our lives. Divorce, death, and illness can all usher in a cloud of doubt. *Why am I going through this? Have I believed something that is not true? Is God really good?* And when the questions come, we must not ignore them. We cannot wish them away with simplistic faith or pious rhetoric. Nor can we simply give them free rein to control our thinking. Such questions must be dealt with honestly. Are they coming from our circumstances or from real doubts about God?

It is critical to acknowledge that external factors *can* play a part in our internal churning, because we may mistake doubt for what is really just anger or hunger or even exhaustion. And while those things can affect how we feel about our faith, they are not doubt—they are just feelings. Feelings will fade as we take care of ourselves and receive reassurance from other believers. This can be a great comfort to our hearts. You may fear you are doubting your faith, but a friend may suggest not tackling a problem until you've had a good night's rest, which could be your greatest need. And such a friend may be right.

But sometimes the morning doesn't bring peace, relief, or comfort; it brings new questions and doubts. Whether we are in a physical prison or a prison of suffering or pain, we are vulnerable to wondering the same things that John the Baptist wondered. *Did I get it wrong? Should I be looking for someone else? Perhaps what I have believed is not worth believing, especially if this is where it leads me. How can I know for certain that my picture of Christ is even correct?*

For John, there might have been old wounds that contributed to his questions. While he didn't care much what people said about him now, what if that hadn't always been the case? John was a different and unique kind of person from the very beginning. Perhaps earlier in his life it bothered him what people would say to him and his parents about the way he dressed or the way he spoke or what he ate. And now, isolated in his lonely cell, he began to wonder if people were right and maybe he was a little crazy. Maybe more than questioning Jesus, he was questioning himself.

Or maybe he wondered if he was better off before he met Jesus. Jesus got him in trouble by teaching things like "You shall know the truth, and the truth will set you free." John could have easily thought, *I told the truth and now I am in prison for it. I'm not free at all. It's easy for Jesus to say the truth will set you free, because he's still out there teaching and healing, not locked away in a stinking, rotting cell.*

There is no telling the strength or number of the forces that were pressing down upon John. He had to have been surrounded by other men in the prison who were there for far worse offenses than speaking out against Herod's adultery. Perhaps these men said things like, "You really are nuts. Just shut up about that stupid Herod and his adultery so you can get out of here. Those two were made for each other. Go ahead, be righteous, but just be quiet about it." Or maybe they were harsher in their criticism: "Where is that guy that you think is going to save the world? How come he's never come here? Shouldn't he begin by saving you?"

Whatever the causes of his doubts, they increased to the point where John decided to send his disciples to ask Jesus the question, the question that had been consuming him for weeks, maybe months. John knew he ran the risk of insulting and even offending Jesus with what he wanted to ask. He would be admitting his doubt publicly by just posing the question. How would Jesus respond? What would Jesus think of him now?

Still he had to ask. As do we.

Are You the One?

I need to know.

The opposite of faith is not doubt, but a settled unbelief, just as the opposite of courage is not fear, but cowardice. While fear can lead you to cowardice or to courage, it is an entirely different thing. Doubt is not the absence of faith. On the contrary, we must believe at least partly in something to doubt it at all. Until doubt grows into a conclusion of settled unbelief, it remains faith. So in one sense, doubt can reassure us of our faith and provide us with the opportunity for it to grow and deepen.

But understandably, people of faith never want to ask the question, "Are you the One?" We think that the matter should have been settled by now, and we are embarrassed and confused by our doubt. Like John the Baptist, we don't want to ask the question but we don't want not to ask it. We often feel like we should protect our faith and cordon off our doubt, lest the doubt somehow contaminate the good faith. Doubt can be dangerous; it certainly can lead to unbelief. But the greater danger of doubt lies in ignoring it or pretending that we are not doubting. That, our faith cannot survive.

John faced his doubt and brought the question to the one he believed could answer it. He didn't ask his disciples, "Do you think he's the One?" He didn't ask Jesus a vague, testing question that he didn't really want the answer to, trying to draw him out. With honesty and humility, he brought his fear, reason, and hope out in the open, storm cloud and all, and let it rain. Whatever happened, he knew that ultimately the air would be clear again and he would know.

Are you the One?

Jesus' response is profound and simple: "Tell John what you have seen and heard." He didn't react to John's question negatively at all or even try to reassure John with an emotional response; he wanted John's disciples to tell him the truth—just what they had seen and heard. Knowing John as well as he did, Jesus knew that would be enough.

Honestly, I have wondered, why didn't Jesus just tell him "Yes"? Wouldn't that have settled it? I'm not too sure. If John's doubt was anything like mine, that kind of certainty might have seemed too quick or too flippant to satisfy John. Instead, Jesus relied on his lifelong relationship with John. Knowing that they had both grown up studying the scrolls, Jesus knew that John knew the book of Isaiah. He knew he had studied the prophecies: "Tell him what you see." Jesus appealed to the evidence that surrounded John's disciples, saying, *The blind see, the lame walk, the lepers are cleansed, the deaf hear, the dead are raised, the poor have the gospel preached to them.*

Jesus knew that John would recognize these prophetic words (Isaiah 35:4–6) and that they would speak deeply to the doubts in his heart:

> Say to those who are fearful-hearted,
> "Be strong, do not fear!
> Behold, your God will come with vengeance,
> With the recompense of God;
> He will come and save you."
> Then the eyes of the blind shall be opened,
> And the ears of the deaf shall be unstopped.
> Then the lame shall leap like a deer,
> And the tongue of the dumb sing.
> For waters shall burst forth in the wilderness,
> And streams in the desert.

And another passage still (Isaiah 61:1–2) that John would recognize was the very Scripture that Jesus had read in the temple just months before:

The Spirit of the Lord GOD is upon Me,
Because the LORD has anointed Me
To preach good tidings to the poor;
He has sent Me to heal the brokenhearted,
To proclaim liberty to the captives,
And the opening of the prison to those who are bound;
To proclaim the acceptable year of the LORD.

Go and tell John the things you have seen and heard: that the blind see, the lame walk, the lepers are cleansed, the deaf hear, the dead are raised, the poor have the gospel preached to them.

Jesus wanted John to hear about the blind and the lame and the deaf and the poor, because he knew John would recognize the fulfillment of Scripture. Jesus trusted John to think on these things, knowing the kind of reassurance it would bring to his mind and heart.

And Jesus was equipping John to deal with doubt. Jesus wanted to prepare him in case another wave of doubt came. John would be able to hold on to the Scripture and to what his own followers had seen, not just something Jesus had said. Doubt can tear apart words as if they were tissue paper. Words can be perceived as emotional or used to quickly satisfy or flatter. Jesus gave John what he needed on the inside to shore up his heart and his mind, knowing that to move past doubt, both must be satisfied. He wanted John to know that others could see what John himself could not see from jail. Jesus was seeking to give John the strength to trust his own faith when he could not clearly see how.

And the last thing Jesus asked John's disciples to tell John was: *Blessed is he who is not offended because of Me.*

Again, Jesus trusted and relied on John's intimate knowledge of the prophecies regarding the One (see also Isaiah 8:14).

This last sentence in Jesus' response to John has also been translated as "Blessed is he to whom I shall not be a stumbling block." Reading this passage felt so personal, almost like a secret communication between the two of them. Jesus was saying, *I am a place of safety for you, John. But I am a stumbling block for most. Don't trip over me—hide in me.*

My guess is that John got the answer he was looking for. My guess is that he listened intently as his disciples reported back what Jesus had done. I can see him sitting on a mat, hearing their words, and looking in their eyes as they described how "the blind see, the lame walk, the lepers are cleansed, the deaf hear, the dead are raised, and the poor have the gospel preached to them." My guess is that tears ran down John's face like rain. My guess is that he slept in peace for the first time in a very long time.

But his nights of peaceful sleep would soon come to an end. The vicious, jealous woman Herodias, with whom Herod had the adulterous affair, was now Herod's wife and she had not forgotten the things John had said. Finally, through the manipulation of her daughter, she would exact her revenge on John.

Herodias's daughter Salome had prepared a dance for the king and his friends. The night of her performance went well, and the king was so pleased he offered to grant Salome any wish, up to half his kingdom. The king must have been surprised and shocked when Salome returned with haste to ask for what she wanted: "I want you to give me at once the head of John the Baptist on a platter." No doubt he could see Herodias's ugly influence behind her wicked request.

It was a tragic ending to John's amazing life, and not what King Herod wanted, as he actually liked to listen to John. (See Mark 6:19–29.)

In the end John and Jesus would both die for speaking the truth to people who not only refused to hear it, but were so offended they wanted it silenced. They "stumbled" badly over this truth—many still do. John came preaching the message that whether you are Herod or homeless, you are a sinner and in need of a Savior. Jesus came to be that Savior, to reveal the powerful truth of God's love for humankind.

It is more than understandable to doubt—many of the same difficulties that pressed down on John are still pressing down on us today—but it is equally imperative to think through our doubts, to weigh the ideas, and finally to strengthen our belief or settle on unbelief. Sometimes we get stuck; we find ourselves in the same place as John. That is when we can follow his example and ask God, "Are you the One?" We can't take this question to those around us; they cannot answer it for us. At some point in matters of faith, every person asks the same question: "Are you the One?"

We have been asking it since the days of Moses, when he

asked God, "Who should I tell the Israelites has sent me?" In essence, "Who are you?" And God told Moses that day to tell the people, "I AM has sent you." He's been saying it ever since.

Personal Reflection

This dramatic encounter between Jesus and the messengers of John the Baptist offers us a simple and life-changing lesson:

Love can handle doubt.

- Do you have doubts about God?

- If hunger or anger or suffering can bring on doubt, as well as other external factors, when do you find yourself most susceptible?

- What do you do with these doubts? How do you go about making big decisions? Through personal experience? Advice? Scripture?

- Are there any beliefs or convictions that have been challenged in your heart and mind because of doubt?

- How could having a distorted picture of God create doubt?

• Does your faith cast light on your problems, or do your problems cast doubt on your faith? Can a person choose the way they want it to be?

Walk in the Way of Love: Be honest about your real questions when they arise. Do not substitute made-up questions that cloud the issues. Read, study, pray, and be committed to seeing some sort of resolution, knowing that you cannot live comfortably in the no-man's-land of doubt. Bring your questions to God. Don't create more confusion by endlessly discussing your doubt with people who haven't worked out their own beliefs yet. Trust that God's love can handle doubt that seeks to be resolved, and know that it can actually help you grow in faith.

Recommended Reading: God in the Dark by Os Guinness (Crossway, 1996)

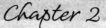

Chapter 2

A Tale of Two Sisters

A dramatic encounter with Mary and Martha

Life-Changing Lesson:

Love refuses to compare

Biblical Passage:

Luke 10:38–42

Now it happened as they went that He entered a certain village; and a certain woman named Martha welcomed Him into her house. And she had a sister called Mary, who also sat at Jesus' feet and heard His word. But Martha was distracted with much serving, and she approached Him and said, "Lord, do You not care that my sister has left me to serve alone? Therefore tell her to help me."

And Jesus answered and said to her, "Martha, Martha, you are worried and troubled about many things. But one thing is needed, and Mary has chosen that good part, which will not be taken away from her." (Luke 10:38–42)

*O*kay, I have to talk fast—not that I don't already, but I am on a very short break. My name is Tammie Jean Smith, and I'm a coffee shop waitress at Bob's Diner.

Last year, I joined a Bible study. Now this is a miracle, y'all. Not that I joined a Bible study, but that after a month they still let me come. The first two weeks I asked so many questions, three people dropped out. I have now learned not to say everything I think, and I have six months of perfect attendance under my belt.

And then, what do you know but last week, the leader of our Bible study asked me if I would take next week and teach the class! You could have knocked me down with a peacock feather. Me, Tammie Jean Smith, teaching a Bible study? There are a whole lot of people in this county who would never believe that! And one of them is telling you this story.

So after giving it a little thought and a lot of prayer, like "Lord, help me help you," I picked the story of Mary and Martha for my turn at the Bible study. Without a doubt, they are the most famous sisters in all of the Bible, and probably my favorites, because sometimes, as sisters, they had a little problem with each other—just like me and my sister.

Sylvia Mae is my "younger sibling." That's what she likes to be called—not "my little sister the brat" or other endearing names I had for her when we were growin' up.

Did I mention that I am from the South? I know I've lost my accent, but you can tell by all the double names in our family. When I was little, all I wanted was to be named Beth—and that's all—not Bethany Louise, like my cousin, just plain Beth.

Anyhoo—I have got to talk fast. I told Bob I was taking out the trash.

The "sistas," as I like to call them because it makes me feel hip, lived in a house with their brother, Lazarus (as in "Lazarus, come forth," but that's not till later). At this particular moment, Jesus was just visiting in their house and teaching the people. It seems like their house was the place to hang out; all the folks would come there, and Jesus would talk to them. Don't you know Martha got tired of that?

"Mary, why does he always have to come here? I was gonna watch *Desperate Housewives* on TV tonight. Now I gotta watch *60 Minutes*."

I'm just teasing. It probably wasn't like that at all, really—I'm sure they both loved Jesus, and it's obvious that Jesus loved them. But it might have been a little bit of a burden on Martha, because she and Mary were as different as salt and pepper. And I can relate to that. I'm older than Sylvia Mae, so sometimes we just chalk up our disagreements to our difference in age. But there is less than two years' difference between us—Momma didn't count her days right, and when she and Daddy . . . but that is another story. I gotta keep going.

Now, I am no Bible scholar, but I know one thing: Martha was in a huff. No one was pitchin' in, and everything was falling on her. *Why do I always have to do all the work? Don't you think I want to hear Him too? How come everyone else gets to come over here, but no one—not even my own sister—lifts a finger to help me?*

I'm just guessing that's how she might have felt. After all, it was Martha's house. The Bible doesn't tell us if Mary contributed to the house payment, or just Martha's workload. Mary might have gotten distracted, sat down for just a minute. That's just how it is with Sylvia Mae. I swear that girl could sit down to watch a commercial at nine in the morning and be there until *Jeopardy*.

And so Martha spotted Mary, not on her way to the kitchen to help, but actually seated at the feet of Jesus. *What is she doing?*

And what about everybody else? I bet she wanted to tap a couple of them on the shoulder and say, "Hey, this event isn't for you. Get in the kitchen and help me. Don't you think I want to hear what he has to say too? He's my friend, too, but some of us have to work around here."

I'm just guessing that's how she might have felt.

Well, actually, I completely relate to Martha. And it's not just 'cause of our sisters. My momma should have just named me Martha Jean. It's hard for me to stop working. I can always think of more things that need to be done.

Other people might wonder what Martha was so stressed about, but not me. Remember the loaves and the fishes? They had a front-row seat on that one, and Martha might have started thinking, *Just because he did that once doesn't mean he's going to do that again. The last time he came to our house, we had wall-to-wall people and no miracle. I'm just not willing to run out of food. We have to have more than enough just in case, or people will talk. It's not like you can count on him performing a miracle.*

But back to the Bible: Martha said, "Lord, do You not care that my sister has left me to serve alone?"

I can't believe she had the nerve to ask him that! And then look, she didn't even let the Lord answer. She just went right on and told him what to do!

"Tell her to help me."

Martha wanted to serve God, but only in an advisory capacity.

Look at the way her bossiness came out. "Lord, tell her to help me." Even a control freak like me can recognize that. Martha wanted the Lord on her side. She'd probably been asking Mary for years to get up and help her, but it never worked. I wouldn't be surprised if Sylvia Mae—I mean Mary—responded that she was an adult and she was going to do what she durn well pleased. And what Mary wanted to do in that moment was sit and soak it in.

I have wondered, what was Jesus teaching about that day? What do you think Mary was so captivated by? Why did she stop and sit down at his feet? Maybe he was saying, "Come unto me, all who are weary and heavy laden...." Or "You shall know the truth and the truth will set you free."

And Martha just had to interrupt him to tattle on Mary.

"She's not doing anything. Don't you see me, Jesus? Yoo-hoo! Don't you recognize how hard I'm working for you?"

If there was one person I would not want to play the martyr for, it would be Jesus, honey. Know your audience.

> And Jesus answered and said to her, "Martha, Martha, you are worried and troubled about many things [to say the least]. But one thing is needed, and Mary has chosen that good part, which will not be taken away from her."

His knowing love and chiding probably sent her back to the kitchen in tears. I know it would have me. What is wrong with me? Why did he say I was worried and troubled? Why *am* I worried and troubled? Why can't I just enjoy myself without having to take care of everything and everybody? Why couldn't I just sit down in the living room and listen to him? What am I so afraid of? Of people not having enough to eat? Of the napkins not being laid out just right? Or if I stop working, no one will like me? I won't like me? Heck, I don't like me.

I'm just guessing that's how she might have felt.

Maybe she started putting the pieces together and talking to herself. *Let the truth set you free, Martha. Sit at his feet. He's not going to love you more for all your work for him, especially if you're really just doing it for yourself.*

But here's the beauty of it. Jesus was being real gentle in helping Martha see her own issues. He didn't say very much, but he knew she would take it deep inside because she was a control freak. Now, I know what you're thinking: the Bible is so outdated and you wish it would really address the issues that modern women face today. Ha!

Anyway, Jesus wanted Martha to stop workin' and stewin' on the inside. If Martha really *wanted* to be in the kitchen, she never would have gotten on Mary's case. But Martha wasn't happy in the kitchen. She acted like she wanted to be in the living room, listening to the teaching. What she really wanted was *Mary* in the kitchen. Control freaks want everyone else to do what they want them to do, especially if they don't really want to do it themselves.

At least, I'm just guessing that's how they might feel.

But Jesus, he saw right through Martha. He wanted her to stop comparing herself to Mary.

Lord, look at her just sitting there—she's not helping me one bit— She looks to the left and to the right. You can almost hear her whining, *Don't you care that she has left me to do all the work?* Sniff, sniff.

Martha was revealing one of the biggest problems we have as women: comparison. We compare everything: prices, clothes, houses, husbands, rear-end sizes . . . Men do not do this. They just feel better than everybody else for absolutely no reason at all. Can you imagine if a man said to his friend, "Well, tell ya the truth, Bubba, I think those jeans do make your butt look big." I'm not man bashing; I'm just telling the truth.

It's the Marthas of the world who created comparison shopping. We don't want to know what this cereal costs; we want to know what all cereals cost and what you paid for the cereal you bought. We not only want to know what size jeans we wear; we want to know what size jeans that woman over there is wearing. Is she my size, or is she smaller than me? Well, now I have to hate her. It's not pretty, and I'm not proud of it; I'm just trying to help us get to the bottom of this story. No pun intended.

But have you ever noticed that we only compare up? We don't compare down. Martha wouldn't compare herself to other women who had it much worse, and I don't either, for that matter. No, we Marthas only have "the obsessive eye" on the women who have it better—or those we think have it better.

I don't think either of the sisters was married, though Martha may have been at one time, 'cause she had the house.

And it would not be hard to guess that she was comparing all that too. That's what we do. If we're single, we want to be married, and when we're married, we want to be single. Whatever we don't have is what we want. You know why single women weigh less, right? It's because single women look at what's in the fridge and go to bed. Married women look at what's in the bed and go to the fridge.

I'm just kidding, y'all. I have a wonderful husband, Walter. I met him at the diner about five years ago, and he loves me like crazy. But that doesn't always keep my eyes from studying what's going on in everybody else's life. I'm not proud of that; I'm just telling you the truth. This is why women love magazines—because we can focus on what someone else is doing or wearing or saying or where they are going or what they are buying.

And speaking of that, have you noticed that women's magazines have been saying the same thing our whole lives? It's true. I looked at a magazine in my basement from 1972, and there were the same promises on the front cover: *How to Have It All*, *Ten Surefire Ways to Be Better*, *How to Be What Your Man Wants*. You would think if a man could be satisfied sexually, we could have figured it out by now and moved on! But no, every issue is full of the same things over and over, year after year—does anybody else think that's strange?

And Jesus goes right to the heart of our condition when he says to Martha, "STOP." Well, sort of.

We can't be self-righteous. Jesus will not allow it. We can work, we can sacrifice, we don't have to sit at his feet all the time like Mary, but we do have to be free. We have to believe enough in what we're doing to do it by ourselves. If someone has to join us doin' it, then we need the praise too much and that won't work. We can't pull others away from the feet of Jesus to do the work we want them to do. Don't ask me how I know this; just trust me that I do.

Jesus was sort of saying, "You may choose to be there in the kitchen, but you can't come out here and ask me to scold Mary for her choice when you could have made the same choice. Relax, Tammie Jean. Not from your work—just stop the churning inside. Stop comparing and looking at what everybody else is doing or not doing."

What would that do to you, to not look at others to the left or the right and to look only at yourself?

I'm still thinking on that. But most of us know it's hard to stop all that comparing. I feel it with other mothers. Hope is only two years old, but already I feel the pressure to have the best teachers, the best ballet classes, the best doctors. . . . Is that really about our children or is it about us? We want our daughters to accept themselves, but we don't accept ourselves, because we can't accept anything but what we think is "the best." But Jesus said that when you are working so hard to have the best, you just might not recognize the best when it is right in your own living room.

I am no Bible scholar, but I am a recovering perfectionist. Of course, that means I'm trying not to recover too well, so that makes it really hard to know when I finally get there—if I ever do . . .

I guess in the end I'm really after the same thing Aretha Franklin was after in *The Blues Brothers*. Remember how she was working in that diner when Jake and Elwood came in and she jumped up on that counter singing, "Freedom, freedom, freedom, freedom . . ."? Now my boss, Bob, would have me arrested, but I don't care. I know something he doesn't.

A year ago, Walter got some stock options in his company. Neither of us even knew that Dow Jones wasn't a real person, but we sure do now. So Bob can fire me if he wants to; I don't need the money. I'm still working 'cause I like what I do. I can serve people from the kitchen and even worship God in there too.

Well, y'all pray for me. I'm not sure what I'm gonna say in that Bible study—but I figure the Lord will help me.

"I'm coming, Bob. You're gonna know the truth soon, and the truth is gonna set me free!"

Freedom, freedom, freedom . . .

Personal Reflection

This dramatic encounter between Jesus and Martha offers us a simple and life-changing lesson:

Love refuses to compare.

- How often do you compare yourself to others? With what or with whom are you most tempted to compare?

- It would be easy to think that it was Martha's work that Jesus was rebuking, but what was underneath her work? What is underneath your work for God? Is work bad?

- Should each of us sit at the feet of Jesus all day long? Is that what you think he wanted from Martha?

- Why do you think self-righteousness is something Jesus constantly pointed out?

- Does a person know when he or she is self-righteous? What do other people notice about a self-righteous person?

- What do you think is behind our culture's breathless pursuit of "the best"?

Walk in the Way of Love: Stop comparing yourself to others or others to yourself. Ask the spirit to help you recognize when you are doing it. Identify what your measuring sticks are and then intentionally lay them down. Instead, seek the "good part" that will not be taken away from you. Find and embrace the peace that comes from sitting at Jesus' feet and listening to his words of love. Put aside your agendas and your "serving" mode just to see what happens as you receive.

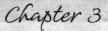
Chapter 3

The Girl of the Tombs

A dramatic encounter for a man who cut himself

Life-Changing Lesson:

Love can change your name

Biblical Passage:

Mark 5:1–20

Then they came to the other side of the sea, to the country of the Gadarenes. And when He had come out of the boat, immediately there met Him out of the tombs a man with an unclean spirit, who had his dwelling among the tombs; and no one could bind him, not even with chains, because he had often been bound with shackles and chains. And the chains had been pulled apart by him, and the shackles broken in pieces; neither could anyone tame him. And always, night and day, he was in the mountains and in the tombs, crying out and cutting himself with stones.

When he saw Jesus from afar, he ran and worshiped Him. And he cried out with a loud voice and said, "What have I to do with You, Jesus, Son of the Most High God? I implore You by God that You do not torment me."

For He said to him, "Come out of the man, unclean spirit!" Then He asked him, "What is your name?"

And he answered, saying, "My name is Legion; for we are many." Also he begged Him earnestly that He would not send them out of the country.

Now a large herd of swine was feeding there near the mountains. So all the demons begged Him, saying, "Send us to the swine, that we may enter them." And at once Jesus gave them permission. Then the unclean spirits went out and entered the swine (there were about two thousand); and the herd ran violently down the steep place into the sea, and drowned in the sea.

So those who fed the swine fled, and they told it in the city and in the country. And they went out to see what it was that had happened. Then they came to Jesus, and saw the one who had been demon-possessed and had the legion, sitting and clothed and in his right mind. And they were afraid. And those who saw it told them how it happened to him who had been demon-possessed, and about the swine. Then they began to plead with Him to depart from their region.

And when He got into the boat, he who had been demon-possessed begged Him that he might be with Him. However, Jesus did not permit him, but said to him, "Go home to your friends, and tell them what great things the Lord has done for you, and how He has had compassion on you." And he departed and began to proclaim in Decapolis all that Jesus had done for him; and all marveled. (Mark 5:1–20)

*P*eople have been cutting themselves for a long time. Many think it is a new problem—not realizing it has been around for centuries. But today's sad trend finds blades in the hands of teenage girls. I had read extensively on the issue, but I hadn't dealt with anyone in therapy until I met Allison. She stepped into my office while her mother waited anxiously in the room outside.

She was very pretty and small. I first noticed the little cuts on her feet. She was wearing flip-flops, and when she noticed me looking, she confirmed my thinking: "I'm a cutter."

I just nodded.

"When things get too much for me to handle, I take a little blade and make a cut." She shrugged. "It makes me feel better, but it freaks most people out."

"It doesn't freak me out, Allison, but how long have you been cutting?"

"A couple of years, I guess." She couldn't hold my gaze. "But lately it's gotten a little worse."

My eyes could verify she was telling me the truth as I saw her arms and a prominent cut on her neck. "Whose idea was it for you to come and see me?"

Her quick glance toward the door revealed the truth, but she immediately looked down and offered, "Mine, I guess."

I could only hope that she shared in the responsibility of the decision to seek help, so that she would participate in the process.

"Have a seat, if you'd like."

People wonder why anyone, especially a child, would *choose* to inflict physical damage on him- or herself, but only because they cannot imagine themselves doing such a thing. They dismiss self-injury as senseless or irrational behavior, and certainly it does seem that way at first glance. But people do things for reasons that make sense to them. I get paid to figure out those reasons. I just wish figuring it out would be enough to change it.

"Allison, why do you think you cut yourself?"

"I did it the first time because I wanted to cry. We aren't really allowed to cry at our house. My father has a very short temper, and if you make noise that will annoy him, like crying, he gets mad."

"So you don't cry? Just so you don't upset your Dad?"

"It's not that I can't cry; it's just best that I don't. I guess I cry through the bleeding maybe. Like my body cries for me."

"Have you ever heard the story in the Bible about a man who cut himself?"

She shrugged her shoulders. She hadn't heard the story, and it seemed she didn't really care to.

As a psychologist, I am very careful with the subject of faith. Often its misinterpretation, or even manipulation, is what brings people to see me. But as a Christian and a person of science, I am free in my practice to utilize some of the powerful ways Christianity and science reinforce each other to aid in a person's health and well-being. Science alone cannot teach the heart to love nor can it heal the heart of pain. But love can use science in its service to reach deep inside the soul and psyche, bringing its power and life-changing stability.

"He lived among the tombs, this man—among the dead—which was where he felt most comfortable, because he was alive but he was not living. There were no razors in his day, so he used stones. He listened to the voices in his head telling him to do terrible things to himself, and he gave in to them. *The pain will feel good to you*, they whispered, *It hurts, doesn't it? Make yourself bleed.* And he did. And he cried out day and night."

Allison's head was down, and it was hard to tell if she was listening or just waiting for me to finish. I've learned with teenagers sometimes there is no difference.

"He was very strong, this man of the tombs. They tried to bind him with chains or rope, but nothing could hold him. He ripped them apart because he himself was ripped apart. He cut himself because he himself was cut, and he was searching for a way to make the outside match the inside." I stopped talking for a minute as the reality of her story met the history of his. "Maybe his dad never let him cry either."

I could see I'd reached something inside her.

Her head was still down, but she swallowed hard. "Sometimes I cut just to see my blood, so that I know I am still alive."

My mind was racing and my heart was so drawn to her. What was causing this young girl to feel so dead inside? Where was this pain coming from? Who had cut her on the inside?

One thing became clear. Allison didn't want to kill herself. She cut her little feet to *keep* from killing herself, but why did she want to? She desperately wanted to control this pain. She wanted to be in charge of when she would hurt and when she would bleed because she couldn't control when other people hurt her, when other people cut her on the inside and made her bleed.

"Can I tell you a little more about that story?" I asked.

She nodded, and for the first time since coming into my office, she looked at me. I smiled at her.

"The man of the tombs saw Jesus coming and began shouting things at him. But as Jesus got closer, he asked the man, 'What is your name?' It seems like a simple question, doesn't it? But I wonder how long it had been since anyone had asked him that. The man answered, 'Legion, for we are many.' Do you know what a legion is?"

"A lot."

"Yep. Smart girl." I then saw that maybe a little smile had formed on the corner of her mouth.

"I'm not sure," I continued, "but I don't think that was the name his mother picked out for him when he was a baby. He called himself Legion because he had a lot of names inside of him. Horrible names he had given to himself, names like "crazy" and "psychotic." You already told me one of your names before I even asked you—you said, 'I'm a cutter.' What other names do you have for yourself, Allison?"

"I don't know."

"Sure you do; you use them all the time. What else do you call yourself?"

"Stupid, maybe."

"What else?"

"Ugly."

"Mmm. Not so good. What about sad or hurt?"

"Yeah. Sometimes when I hear them fighting or him yelling, I get really upset. I feel sad for my mom, and I am kinda mad at my dad. I think about all this stuff and then I just go in the bathroom and start cutting. And I feel better. Sometimes I wish I didn't feel better. I know it's screwed up, but I feel this relief. But then it's gone again, and I'm sad."

"And I heard angry."

"Yeah, that, too, I guess."

"You guess?"

"Yeah—I kinda get mad a lot."

"At who?"

"Myself. Sometimes I cut as a way of punishing myself for what I've done wrong."

"What kind of things have you done wrong?"

"I don't know—lots of things."

"Like wanting to cry?"

I was sure that Allison wasn't perfect, and I was sure that she was capable of angry fits or sullen moods or leaving her clothes strewn about her room, but this child was taking the punishment for a lot of wrong that didn't belong to her. At fourteen, what could she have done that would warrant being punished in this way? For whose wrongs was she punishing herself?

"What about names you've been called?"

"Lazy. Dumb. Funny looking. Forgetful."

It was easy for her to say those words; it was as if she didn't even feel it. No wonder she felt that she was dying. "Does your dad say those things to you?"

Her silence was enough to make me want to cry. The puzzle was coming together and the picture wasn't a pretty one. Allison was terrified of what would happen to her if she were honest about her feelings. She didn't even know what that meant, just that it was "better" if she didn't tell the truth.

Teenage girls face enormous pressure to split into false selves. They are often faced with the choice to be true to self and risk abandonment or compromise self to be more acceptable. For Allison, the choice wasn't happening at school, as it does for many girls. The fork in the road between her real self and her false self was at home.

I have treated many girls for anorexia and bulimia—trying to keep them from sacrificing their real selves to some cultural ideal that might cost them their lives. Or I talk to them about not giving in to the pressures of sex because of the internal compromise that takes place when they put the perceived need or want of a boy above their own needs. Allison was facing the same choice. But instead of having to say no to the pressure of her peers or an image in the culture, she was going to have to face her father, and I knew that this might be her greatest fear.

My thoughts turned to Allison's mother sitting in the outer room, and I wondered what she was thinking. Was she out there flipping through a magazine? Was she on her cell phone gossiping with a friend? Or was she seriously contemplating the role she might be playing in her daughter's drama? I could only hope it was the latter.

Too many women just want to save their marriages or rescue their kids from problems, but they have no idea who they are. If I ask a woman what she really needs, often she has no idea what to say to me. I find many women confused by the question itself. "Me? I don't figure into this equation." They couldn't be more wrong.

Especially when it comes to their daughters. A mother may find herself unable to help her little girl answer her teenage questions because after thirty years of asking them herself, she still has no answers.

How important are looks and popularity?

Can I be honest with my husband or my friends and still be loved?

Can I be responsive without being responsible for everything?

If the mother is unable to separate who she really is from who she feels she is "supposed to be," the "supposed to be" has already won. Internally she has given up because she believes her world would fall apart if she expressed her true thoughts, beliefs, or emotions. Perhaps Allison's mother had resigned herself to being a quiet, sad wife to a verbally abusive husband.

But her daughter was paying the price.

"Allison, have you thought that maybe you are cutting yourself because of your parents?" I thought she might look horrified by the suggestion, but as she seemed to consider what I was saying, her chin began to tighten to stop her lip from quivering. I decided to keep going.

"You don't want to be mad at your parents, do you?" Allison

shut her eyes tight and wrapped her arms around her waist. "So you just take it out on yourself. You just keep trying to make everything okay, to pay for all that is wrong, but you're paying with your own blood."

Many self-injurers have enormous amounts of anger inside. Afraid to express it outwardly, perhaps because of another angry person in the house, they hurt themselves as a way of venting these feelings, at the same time punishing themselves for having feelings they don't want to have. Allison preferred to feel the pain of cutting over the pain of confronting all she couldn't understand in her own life.

If she allowed herself to feel the rage and anger of living with a violent man she could not control, it might be overwhelming—and she might make matters worse. So instead she just made her little cuts to cope. In her mind, it was a lot easier. And in some ways, I'd have to agree with her reasoning in the short term; but the truth was, it was getting worse. Someday she'd have to cut her own heart out to survive this man.

"What if I told you I think your father is destructive?" I was being very careful but intentional. "He's not a bad man, but he is hurting you and your family. Would you agree with that?" She was fighting hard to hold back the tsunami of emotions

The Girl of the Tombs   47

that were coming from the earthquake my questions had caused. I was afraid she might bite through her lip.

"He's not here, Allison. You can cry. And you should. You can scream if you want to, and you can make all the noise in the world. I won't be annoyed or angry with you."

The floodgate opened, and the tears came through like a mighty rushing river, and that little girl sobbed and sobbed. She finally let herself feel the real pain of her situation. Her father was angry and there was nothing she could do about it. It wasn't her fault and she couldn't pay the price for him. Her mother had tried for years and lived with an overwhelming sadness—a sadness that wasn't Allison's fault either.

"You can't save them." I waited until I hoped that she could hear me way down inside. "You know why? It's not your job. You can't do it. You know what your job is? Your job is just to be a fourteen-year-old girl who likes whatever you like, ice cream, pizza, shopping at the mall. You are a daughter to your parents, a friend to your friends—but you are no one's savior. It's not your job.

"I don't know whose pain that man in the Bible carried inside himself—a lot of people's, I imagine—but Jesus took it away from him. It didn't belong to him—it was too much for him. Jesus cast all that mess into a herd of pigs, and the pigs ran off the cliff and killed themselves."

Allison looked directly at me.

"Says a lot, doesn't it? It's too much for one person."

She nodded, fresh tears rolling slowly down her cheeks.

"It's too much. Jesus can be your parents' Savior; you can just be their daughter."

"It hurts so bad." She was doubled over in her chair, and I wondered if she was looking at her feet.

"I know it does, Allison. And you probably want to cut right now, just to not have to feel this pain."

She nodded with her head down. "The best thing you can do is just cry and cry and cry. Can you feel your tears? You're alive in there. You're alive. No blood. No more blood."

My heart was just breaking. I wanted a better life for Allison, a life of freedom and joy. A life she would not have until she found a better way to cope with her parents.

In the biblical story, the people were more concerned with the pigs than they were with the man. They were appalled and worried over the loss of a commodity. Pigs were the lowest of creatures, the dirtiest of animals, and the people were more worried about what happened to them than what had happened in this man's life. I wish I could say a lot has changed in two thousand years, but Allison's mother had already revealed a question asked by Allison's father: "How much is it gonna cost to get her to stop doing this?" His daughter was cutting herself, and he was worried about the money.

"We'll need to schedule some time with your parents, Allison." More tears rolled down her cheeks.

When they saw the man who had been possessed clothed and sitting in his right mind, they were afraid. Why *then*? They were more comfortable with his unclean spirits than with his sanity. Allison's parents had not recognized what kind of pain they were putting on their daughter because they had refused to acknowledge their own destructive patterns. Maybe they had no idea their little girl was taking it all inside. I wondered what would happen in their lives when Allison began to put some of that pain where it really belonged. Her father might find himself more afraid than he was of her cutting. And the cost to him might be much more expensive than dollars.

People thought the man of the tombs was crazy. He thought he was, too—until God interrupted the terrible conversation going on in his head with a new voice, the voice of Love. That voice spoke the world into existence, it calmed the sea, and it calmed the raging emotions inside the man of the tombs, giving him a new existence.

"You have been listening in on a terrible conversation for way too long, Allison, a conversation that has only served to make you feel worthless and angry. But there is a voice of love, a conversation of the ages that we can listen to for strength and comfort. God's love doesn't take away our rocks; it takes away our need to use those rocks to hurt ourselves. He gives us a new name."

Her eyes met mine. "Your name is not cutter, and your name is not anger. Your name is not worthless. Those names will fade in the light of his love. Your name is Allison. Your name is daughter. Your name is safe. Your name is loved.

"May I give you a hug?" I asked, rising and moving toward her. She stood and opened her arms as we embraced and formed a bond that would never be broken. Much had happened in our short time together, and I could only hope its results would last a lifetime.

I knew there would still be quite a journey ahead, but I felt certain that she would trust me as we went forward. There would be some hard days for Allison, and for her parents, but I felt that the course of her life had been redirected. She had opened her heart to strong, divine love, and I prayed her little feet and heart would be safe from her destructive blades because this love had changed her name.

Personal Reflection

This dramatic encounter between Jesus and the demon-possessed man offers us a simple and life-changing lesson:

Love can change your name.

• What names do you have for yourself? Where did you get them?

• Are there instruments you use or have used in the past to inflict pain on yourself? (Don't forget that things like food, drugs, alcohol, work, or even church activity can be weapons too.) Why did you choose them?

• How do you speak to yourself on the inside? What are the tone and purpose of your self-talk?

• Do you have any unresolved anger in your heart?

• How do you think God sees you?

Walk in the Way of Love: Listen to the voice of the God who asked the demon-possessed man what his name was. Redefine your names according to how you believe he sees you *by faith*, not by your feelings. Write those names on a piece of paper, or somewhere you can see them regularly. Lay down any destructive tool that you use to hurt yourself and look to the wounds of Christ as a substitute for your wounds. Say to yourself, "Christ took this pain and these cuts, so I don't have to do this to myself, so I don't have to save anyone else." Trust that his love has forever changed your name.

Chapter 4

Stretch Out Your Hand

A dramatic encounter with a man
with a withered hand

Life-Changing Lesson:

Love goes deeper than religion

Biblical Passage:

Luke 6:5–11

Now it happened on another Sabbath, also, that He entered the synagogue and taught. And a man was there whose right hand was withered. So the scribes and Pharisees watched Him closely, whether He would heal on the Sabbath, that they might find an accusation against Him. But He knew their thoughts, and said to the man who had the withered hand, "Arise and stand here." And he arose and stood. Then Jesus said to them, "I will ask you one thing: Is it lawful on the Sabbath to do good or to do evil, to save life or to destroy?" And when He had looked around at them all, He said to the man, "Stretch out your hand." And he did so, and his hand was restored as whole as the other. But they were filled with rage, and discussed with one another what they might do to Jesus. (Luke 6:5–11)

*T*his scene might as well have been set in a courtroom, for all the drama that was going on. It was like a first-century episode of *Law and Order* that would change the lives of all who were there. We can see the basic facts of the story, but what really happened that day?

Jesus entered the synagogue on the Sabbath, and he began teaching. Among those who were listening to him was a man whose right hand was withered. We don't know why he was there that day; perhaps he was a "regular." Or perhaps it was his first time in the synagogue because of the shame of his withered hand. It is also possible that he was invited to attend the synagogue by a group of religious leaders who had an agenda.

Luke doesn't tell us why the man's hand was withered. What had happened to him? Maybe an early wound or injury had slowly taken the life out of it. Perhaps his hand had been that way since his birth. We just don't know. What we do know is it had stopped growing, it had shriveled, and it was no longer useful to him. And in religious circles, the only thing his withered hand could hold was shame and embarrassment. It is likely that he'd been ridiculed, rejected, and perhaps even tortured. But in the synagogue, in the midst of everyone there that day, in the midst of all the others whose hands were whole and complete, Jesus saw him.

The account tells us that the scribes and Pharisees watched Jesus closely. They had seen him "see" someone before. They knew a dramatic encounter of some sort was about to take place. This might even be their chance to accuse him publicly of breaking the law if he actually tried to heal the man.

Perhaps the Pharisees pushed the man forward a little, to the front, like bait. *Here he is, one of your broken ones! What are you going to do with him? You usually heal them, don't you? You can't resist mocking us with your miracles, but we're ready this time. Go ahead, work your magic.*

Perhaps their hands were a little clammy as they watched Jesus look upon the man. Would he dare heal on the Sabbath and break the law right there in the synagogue?

They hoped he would. This would be their chance.

But Jesus saw more than just the man with the withered

hand that day. He turned his gaze to the hearts of the Pharisees, and they looked just like the man's hand—withered and useless. Their hearts had stopped growing a long time ago and were now shriveled up and dry. Maybe just as with the man, a wound or injury had taken the life out of them. Perhaps just the hardness of unyielding religion had stunted their growth and made them small. And just like the man, the religious leaders tried to keep their withered hearts tucked away from the penetrating stare of Jesus.

Then Jesus said to the man who had the withered hand, "Arise and stand here." What must have been going on inside the head and the heart of this man? Was he immediately excited? Or was he terrified? If he was there on the side of the Pharisees and had agreed to be a pawn for them, it's possible that he never thought anything would really happen. Perhaps he was there on his own, just coming to synagogue like he always did on the Sabbath. Had he seen the power struggle going on and was he smart enough not to want to be placed in the middle of it?

Whatever else was going on, Jesus was speaking to *him*. "Arise and stand here."

He never thought it would come to this. *I don't want to be up there in front of anyone. Please don't embarrass me. I only wanted to come to hear what you had to say. I'm not really welcome here. Please don't humiliate me in front of all these people.*

But something moved the man forward, and he arose and stood next to Jesus.

A hush fell over this synagogue "courtroom." If Jesus healed the man, the Pharisees would accuse him right then and there of breaking the Sabbath laws. They might even take center stage and ask the people, "What kind of Jew is he, if he works in our synagogue?" If he didn't heal the man, the crowd just might turn on Jesus for calling the man up there and being so cruel. *What happened to his power? Does he really think he is a holy man?*

The crowd wanted a show, a miracle, a spectacle. The Pharisees wanted a conviction and public humiliation of this heretical teacher. And Jesus wanted to do what he had always done— reveal the heart of God to people who didn't get it.

The man with the withered hand stood up in front of them all, but Jesus didn't address him first, choosing instead to speak to the Pharisees. He asked them a simple question. "Is it lawful on the Sabbath to do good or to do evil, to save life or to destroy?"

The answer was obvious. No self- or God-respecting Pharisee could say that it was lawful to do evil or to destroy anything on the Sabbath, but what was he getting at when he talked about saving life and doing good? They knew he was trying to turn the tables on them.

It was as if he were saying, *Gentlemen of this self-appointed jury*, "It is not unlawful to do good on the Sabbath. If your sheep fell in a pit, which one of you would not pull him out" (Matthew 12:11). *But which one of you would ever admit that you did? It is never breaking God's law to do good things, no matter when you do them. But it is a mockery of God's law to pretend to be so holy. To have no mercy on one such as this, to use breaking the Sabbath as the excuse for your cruelty is not a reflection of the one true God. You would have me save this man, thereby doing good, but accuse me of disobeying the law—when you have plotted evil against us both and broken the Sabbath by your thoughts and deeds.*

Jesus had a way of leaving people speechless.

Luke tells us that Jesus looked around at them all. They said nothing. They must have felt their faces burning as he revealed their intentions. He left them without excuse. It was obvious to all what they had done.

Then he turned his attention to the reason he came, to the man standing beside him, and said, "Stretch out your hand."

Don't you know this man wanted to say to Jesus, *Stretch out my hand? Do you take me for a fool? I cannot. If I could, I would* have stretched it out long before now. Why do you want me to stretch it out? For you to see it? You can see it is useless and deformed; it's ugly. If you're going to heal it, just heal it. Don't make me stretch it out.

Yet Jesus asserted, "Stretch out your hand."

Jesus makes a profound statement in this simple request. It is the stretching that separates faith from fear and self-righteousness and pretense from humility and honesty. And ultimately *stretching* is what took him from woundedness to wholeness. Jesus wasn't interested in the man's good hand. He asked him to stretch out what was shameful and humiliating. It is as if he were saying, *You keep what is whole and pretty; you know what to do with that. But you don't know what to do with what is broken. You despise it; you want to hide it. But I have a better way.*

"Stretch out your hand."

And the man did so, and his hand was restored.

I have no idea how this happened. The Scripture never says that Jesus even touched the man. Jesus simply spoke to him, and he was healed. That is the power of love incarnate.

The religious leaders could accuse Jesus of nothing but talking. However, while he was talking, the man's withered hand became whole. Right in front of everyone's eyes, right in front of the withered hearts.

Then this dramatic encounter gets even more dramatic. Maybe Jesus looked at one of the Pharisees directly and offered him the same opportunity to be healed. The Pharisees could feel the burn of the magnifying gaze of Jesus. *Stretch out your heart. Reach, even if it hurts—stretch past your own righteousness and religion—stretch out your heart and it will be restored.*

"No! I will not! How dare you try to expose me! You are the sham, not me. You are the one misleading people with all this talk of love. Where are the rules? Where is the discipline? You are the one who is wrong."

The Pharisees were filled with rage. They were appalled and offended by what Jesus had done and what he had said. Why? Was it because they could not accuse him of anything and he had accused them of everything? Their religious stronghold was crumbling, and it made them rage inside—just as we want to rage when our sins are revealed. But instead of looking inside themselves, they began discussing with one another what they might do to stop Jesus.

So the broken one—the man with the withered hand who had been so afraid of humiliation—left the synagogue and went home with a new hand, whole and clean. And the "whole" ones—the self-righteous ones with perfect hands—went home broken and humiliated.

I wonder if the man whose hand had been withered was there when Jesus was crucified. Did he stand on the hill that dark day with so many others who had no words for all the good that Jesus had brought into their desperate lives? I wonder if he looked down at his hand that had been restored and wept over the love he had been shown. He couldn't miss the fact that the one who had asked him to stretch out his hand was now stretching out his own.

Alas! and did my Savior bleed? And did my Sovereign die?
Would He devote that sacred head for sinners such as I?
At the cross, at the cross where I first saw the light
And the burden of my heart rolled away,
It was there by faith I received my sight,
And now I am happy all the day!
("Alas! and Did My Savior Bleed?" by Isaac Watts, 1885)

Personal Reflection

This dramatic encounter between Jesus and the man with the withered hand offers us a simple and life-changing lesson:

Love goes deeper than religion.

If there were ever an encounter that seemed to turn religion on its head, it is this one. But look closer: Jesus doesn't set aside religion in this story. He shows deep respect for what religion must mean in order to be true. Religion should lead us to love, but they are not one and the same. Love will always trump religion if they go their separate ways. And love is harder in the long run because it requires sacrifice.

If we harden our hearts in order to "keep the rules," then we're not only missing the point—we're not in the right game. It may look good on the outside, but it is not going to make a difference in people's hearts. At the end of the day, if any religion is only about keeping up appearances, instead of truly loving others, you can know it is not God's way or true religion.

- Which character in this story do you identify with the most?

- Is there something withered, broken, or disfigured in your life that you keep tucked away? Your marriage? A stubborn heart? A broken relationship? A baby lost to abortion?

- Why is it dangerous to despise parts of ourselves? Although it is natural to want to hide those parts, what are the consequences internally?

- What makes a heart wither? What are the indications of a withered heart?

- How can we tell if we are more interested in love or religious rule-keeping? What are the signs?

- Does religion set us up for merely following the rules? Why doesn't that work in relationships?

- What would it look like to stretch out your hand to Jesus?

Walk in the Way of Love: Whether we are broken or self-righteous, the message is the same: Love goes deeper than you can imagine. If your hand is withered, you are welcome to meet God without shame because He loves you. And if you are a religious leader seeking to lead others, lay aside your self-righteousness and let his love go deeper still—knowing that it is truly deeper than any man's agenda, deeper than the rules of any religion, and, thankfully, deeper than anyone's deepest sin.

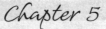
Chapter 5

The Flat Thud of Grace

A dramatic encounter for a woman
caught in adultery

Life-Changing Lesson:

Love can free us from judgment

Biblical Passage:

John 8:2–11

Now early in the morning He came again into the temple, and all the people came to Him; and He sat down and taught them. Then the scribes and Pharisees brought to Him a woman caught in adultery. And when they had set her in the midst, they said to Him, "Teacher, this woman was caught in adultery, in the very act. Now Moses, in the law, commanded us that such should be stoned. But what do You say?" This they said, testing Him, that they might have something of which to accuse Him. But Jesus stooped down and wrote on the ground with His finger, as though He did not hear.

So when they continued asking Him, He raised Himself up and said to them, "He who is without sin among you, let him throw a stone at her first." And again He stooped down and wrote on the ground. Then those who heard it, being convicted by their conscience, went out one by one, beginning with the oldest even to the last. And Jesus was left alone, and the woman standing in the midst. When Jesus had raised Himself up and saw no one but the woman, He said to her, "Woman, where are those accusers of yours? Has no one condemned you?"

She said, "No one, Lord."

And Jesus said to her, "Neither do I condemn you; go and sin no more." (John 8:2–11)

*I*n biblical times there was a way people dealt with sin— rocks. Someone would point out the offender and everyone would come running. Picking up a cold, hard ballot made of stone, they would violently cast their vote against wrong.

But one hot day in the Middle East, a man stepped in front of those rock throwers and changed things forever.

Remember when they brought her in? They threw her down in the dirt and gathered around her angrily with rocks in their hands. Clothes, if she had any, torn off, tears spilling in the dirt in shame, or maybe anger. . . . Where was the man? Was she his heart's love or just the afternoon's activity? Either way, he wasn't there; she was alone and they were on her. They—the self-proclaimed upholders of moral righteousness, the super-pious pillars of the assembly—were armed with their bludgeoning hypocrisy and crowd-pleasing indignation over wrong. She was in big trouble. She'd sinned and been caught, dead-ending her into a circle of angry religious people with rocks in their hands.

Have you ever noticed how good it feels to throw a rock really hard? Your hand feels the weight of the stone, and when you let it fly, there is a tremendous release. Is that what they felt that day? "No," they would yell as they threw. "Wrong! Punish!" They would throw and throw, their fury fueled by each other as much as by the crime, until the one in the center was still. And then they would revel in the grim release of sin avenged. Done.

But the rocks didn't hit the sin. The rocks hit people.

And thousands of years later, they still do.

Oh, we're too sophisticated nowadays to be flinging granite, but the words we throw in judgment and outrage are as hard and cold as any stone of old. And the release we feel when we let them go can be just as exhilarating.

Four teenagers get killed in a drunk-driving accident on a Friday night, and we hurl our rocks: "Well, they shouldn't have been drinking." No, they shouldn't have, but does that ease the guilt and the pain for their parents?

A young woman gets raped leaving a party, and someone says, "She was wearing a short skirt, and she deserves exactly what she got." We drag her into the circle and throw our rocks.

A businessman goes to jail for a poor decision involving other people's money, and we growl, "He can rot in there as far as I'm concerned." Never mind his wife and kids, and we pile the rocks as high as we can.

A woman confronts someone rudely about an indiscretion in her life and later phones a friend to report, "And then I told her exactly what I thought of that sin." Whap! Now that woman will be in no danger of appearing soft on sin—while the woman she hit will wear the bruise.

As we throw, we convince ourselves that if the rock lands in just the right spot, it can knock out something evil. You remember the story of David and Goliath. Plant the rock squarely in the forehead of your foe, and your side wins. If our goal is to kill our enemy, this could be the answer. But if we hope to change a friend's heart, it definitely is not. We can sometimes knock sense into a person with a rock, but we can't knock out sin.

Remember the scene in the movie *Forrest Gump* where Jenny goes back to her childhood house after years of being gone? She stares at the old shack where her daddy—her trusted daddy—would come to her bed at night and use her like a trash receptacle. She picks up a little rock and flings it at the house, breaking a window. She stares and stares as tears start to sting, and then she hurls another rock as hard as she can. She throws and throws, another and another, flinging and crying until she collapses on the ground. Quietly and in his simple way, Forrest pronounces, "Sometimes there just aren't enough rocks."

And there aren't. Jenny was hurling those rocks at something bigger. She threw with all her might, venting years of pain at what that house represented: sin, the blackness that overcomes hearts and makes people unrecognizable as human beings. But there aren't enough rocks in the entire world to beat out sin.

If we actually could throw a rock and hit the evil in the world, we would still run out of rocks before it was all gone. For all the wrongs that have been done to us, there simply are not enough rocks in the world to make it all right.

When Jesus stepped out of the crowd of rock throwers that day and scribbled in the sand, he reminded a group of angry people who wanted to beat the sin out of her that it just wasn't possible. And he wasn't going to let them try just so they could feel better. They could kill her, but it wouldn't solve the bigger problem. And he had come to solve the bigger problem so we wouldn't have to try with our pathetic little rocks.

What did Jesus scribble in the sand that day? The names of men in the crowd who had also slept with her? That would have gotten their attention. Did he just trace patterns in the sand to allow tempers time to cool? Even group vengeance can be stopped if the momentum slows. Or did he write something completely different, such as "She is your daughter"? That would have changed how they felt. Whatever he wrote, he drove it home with these words: "If any one of you is without sin, let him be the first to throw a stone at her."

Silence.

No one could say anything. His words disarmed all their accusations. He cut away the false high ground from under the feet of the self-righteous and for all time leveled the playing field between accused and accusers. He gave those of us who have made the worst choices of our lives a place where it is safe to be broken without fear of being destroyed. He showed us that no matter what, he would stand between our judges and us.

And to those of us who feel as if we have reason and right to throw that rock, he gave the freedom to choose love instead.

These are drop-your-rock moments.

They come at different times for each of us. Maybe you've come running with your rock, only to see your loved one in the center of the circle. And what was so easy to judge before now has a face and eyes. When this happens—when your son tells you he's homosexual or your best friend confesses in agony she's having an affair or your sister tearfully describes her abortion—we have a choice to leave mere theory behind and enter the gritty reality of relationship. As we listen, maybe the anger comes first, our teeth clench, and our grip on the rock tightens. We want to throw it so badly. We want to say exactly what we think of that sin and try to beat it out of them. We've done it a hundred times before, hitting the anonymous sinner, but now it is painfully different.

Love is giving us a chance to choose.

As the tears fall, our fingers loosen, and the rock falls to the ground with the flat thud of grace.

What a sound. That is the sound the woman heard that day in the temple court in Jerusalem. She waited in agony, afraid to hope as she stared at the dirt made into mud by her tears. Hunched over, she waits to be hit hard by the very first rock, but then she hears it drop to the ground. Then another drop . . . and another . . . and another. Then shuffling. Then stillness.

His voice alone broke the silence. "Woman, where are your accusers?"

Eyes downcast, she saw no feet around her, just rocks lying here and there. Still she could not lift her head.

Everyone else was gone. Only he was left.

In a tender voice he asked, "Has no one condemned you?"

She was now at the mercy of God, and he was about to speak. He could have said, "Now that they've all gone, I want to tell you what I think of your behavior." But he didn't. He said, "Neither do I condemn you."

For the first time since the ordeal began, she lifted her head.

When we have done wrong, there is no sweeter moment in all of life than to feel the forgiveness of God. His words told her that it was all right, despite all that was wrong.

And then he said one more thing: "Go and sin no more."

The same Love that called the others to drop their rocks was also giving her a chance to choose: Continue the sickening slavery of wrong, or walk in the freedom of forgiveness. There was a fork in the road for her too.

Grace doesn't just let us off; it sets us free. With one blow it strikes the shackle that binds us, breaking it open so we may walk unfettered in freedom. It promises us a better tomorrow than the today we've made for ourselves. "Go and sin no more."

The "go" is the grace.

The "sin no more" is the cost of staying free.

Could she really "sin no more"? It would depend on which

road she chose with her freedom. Would she go back to her old life, hunting furtively through the streets for the man she'd been with? Or would she feel the powerful strength and dignity that real love and forgiveness had just given her, determine to hold her head high, and never look back?

Have you ever trembled and told a friend something you've done terribly wrong, and then, emotionally hunched over, waited for their stone-cold words of judgment to hit you? But instead you heard the flat thud of grace as their rock hit the ground.

Our rocks will never change the world, only dent and pockmark it with hate and fear. Throwing rocks will never make us more loving. As we clutch and throw our rocks, we reveal our pettiness and our inability to change our own lives. Only when we drop our rocks and choose to love do we become more loving.

So the next time someone trembles in fear and tells you something you really didn't want to know, or you see your sin in someone else's life, or your loved one is braced to feel your stone-cold words, you'll know what to do. Loosen your grip, and listen for the flat thud of grace as you choose love over judgment.

The only one who has the right to throw a rock is the one who has never done any wrong. Ever. The only one who is without blackness in his own heart. The one who has never taken anything from anyone else, never compromised his own standards, never lied, even a little, to make himself look better. There has been only One, and only that One can pick up the rock.

And he did. He became the Rock and took care of our wrong for all time. And he still stands between our accusers and us. And he still lifts our heads and sets us on the path to freedom. When he knelt in the sand that day, just maybe he wrote these words: "My rock is bigger than yours, and I will handle this one."

Rock of ages, cleft for me, let me hide myself in Thee . . .

Personal Reflection

This dramatic encounter between Jesus and a woman caught in adultery (and her accusers) offers us a simple and life-changing lesson:

Love can free us from judgment.

Christ demonstrated this truth for us so clearly. We don't have to wonder what he thinks or what he would do—he showed us that day in Jerusalem—and we can still follow his example, this afternoon or tonight or tomorrow night. God hasn't changed his mind or his ways when it comes to love. Whether we find ourselves in a situation like the woman in the story or like the religious people called to gather around a sinner, love gives us the chance to choose our response carefully.

At first glance, this encounter seems to deal more with the crowd around the woman than with the woman herself. Perhaps it is because so many of us are caught in judgment. We are just as likely to stand in the crowd of accusers as we are to be in the center of the circle, accused. I do think that Christ said plenty to her in the story, indicating that this dramatic encounter occurs for the fallen as well as for those of us who find it easy to judge their fall.

- No one aspires to be judgmental, so why are we?

- Why do most people outside of the Christian faith perceive Christians to be judgmental?

- What things are acceptable to judge? How do we constructively bring about change without judgment?

- Often we can see judgmentalism very clearly in others, but it is much harder to recognize when it lives inside of us. Prayerfully ask yourself these questions:

  —Am I judgmental of others? With my words or in my heart?
  —Do others perceive me as judgmental?
  —Has judging someone ever affected my relationship with them?

- When has it been hardest for you to "drop your rock" of judgment?

• Is "Go and sin no more" a realistic request? What do you think Jesus was getting at?

Walk in the Way of Love: When you are being judged or when you want so badly to judge others, lean into God and look at the depth of his love. His love will release you from judgment, not so you can keep going in the wrong way, but so you can be free to make good decisions with your life and go about living well. His love will also remind you that if you aren't the one in the center of the circle right now, take care before you judge, as you just might be there one day. Choose love confidently, because love is stronger and more powerful than judgment. Drop your rock and listen to the beautiful, flat thud of grace.

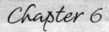

Chapter 6

The Kiss of Death

A dramatic encounter for Judas Iscariot

Life-Changing Lesson:
Love can forgive betrayal

Biblical Passage:
Matthew 26:44–50

So He left them, went away again, and prayed the third time, saying the same words. Then He came to His disciples and said to them, "Are you still sleeping and resting? Behold, the hour is at hand, and the Son of Man is being betrayed into the hands of sinners. Rise, let us be going. See, My betrayer is at hand."

And while He was still speaking, behold, Judas, one of the twelve, with a great multitude with swords and clubs, came from the chief priests and elders of the people.

Now His betrayer had given them a sign, saying, "Whomever I kiss, He is the One; seize Him." Immediately he went up to Jesus and said, "Greetings, Rabbi!" and kissed Him.

But Jesus said to him, "Friend, why have you come?"

Then they came and laid hands on Jesus and took Him. (Matthew 26:44–50)

*J*esus prayed in the Garden of Gethsemane in the early hours of the morning. He had already woken his friends twice to ask them to pray with him, but to no avail. Yet he kept praying. And, as John describes, his intense time of prayer culminated in an overwhelming plea: that his followers would be one, so "that the world may know that You have sent Me, and have loved them as You have loved Me."

Then everything was interrupted. There were sounds of people running and shouting somewhere in the distance. Soon the waking friends could see men with torches and swords and clubs coming toward them as a mob. And then one of the most famous and dramatic encounters in history took place. Some two thousand years later, the words *Judas kiss* remain in our vocabulary—a kiss offered not in love, but in deceit, in betrayal.

Judas had planned everything. "Greetings, Rabbi," he said as he walked toward Jesus and casually offered the kiss. What he had not expected was what happened next as Jesus looked in his eyes and said to him, "Friend, why have you come?"

That wasn't in the plan. Surely Jesus knew why he was there. Jesus knew that Judas wasn't happy; he had even hinted to all the others that Judas would be the one to betray him. Why would he say, "Friend, why have you come?" like nothing was happening? Like he wasn't standing there with a mob of soldiers? Like countless times before when Judas had come to bring news or food—times they had shared together after arriving back from a separate mission, times when Jesus would hail Judas as "Friend."

What was Judas seeing in his eyes? Not confusion—it wasn't even anger, which is what Judas must have been expecting when he arrived with the soldiers in tow. He had guessed Jesus would say something like, "I knew this was coming." Or to the disciples, "It is as I told you. He is the one to betray me." Judas was definitely not expecting, "Friend, why have you come?"

The look in Jesus' eyes was a look Judas would never forget. *Friend? Why?*

It was an opportunity (could there still be time to call this off?), yet at the same time, it was too late. The soldiers were already on each side of Jesus; Judas was pushed out of the way as they grabbed him. Wait! What was it in the Rabbi's eyes?

Betrayal is one of the deepest agonies of the human soul. There is no underestimating the pain of a treacherous kiss offered under the guise of friendship or even love. Only a trusted friend can wound us so deeply. Only a friend has access to kiss you on the cheek. Only a friend gets close enough to betray you. A stranger can stab you in the back, but it takes a friend to break your heart.

For anyone who has been betrayed, the pain is indescribable, and the questions are unavoidable: *Why did they stop believing in me? Why didn't they tell me what they were thinking? Why did they have to do this? Why? Why? Why?*

Why did he sleep with someone else?
Why did she say that about me?
Why did he turn his back on me?

And then our hearts become encased in hurt and the pain turns to anger, and we ask ourselves a different question: *Why did I ever trust them?* There is no shame in believing the best of a person who proved to be false. Still we berate ourselves and feel stupid for "not having seen it coming." Yet even Christ bears the wounds of betrayal. We tend to think only of the marks on his body without considering how his heart was beaten as he went to the cross. He suffered that day—inside and out. Those closest to Jesus were absent in his final hours. One betrayed him straight out; others scattered into the night denying they knew him; and even later on the cross, he felt his heavenly father turn his face away.

Which brings us to the question of why Judas betrayed Jesus. Many people, when asked, simply believe it was for the money. Not that this reasoning isn't valid. Judas was the treasurer of the group and an account in John 12 indicates he took freely from the money box for his own use. Another account reports that Judas was upset to see the woman "waste" the oil on Jesus' feet when it could have been sold, and the money put into the treasury to be used for the poor. Tragically, this was all just pious talk from a greedy heart.

Or if not for the poor, once the money was in the treasury, then perhaps the Revolution could use it? Judas knew they would definitely need all of their resources—manpower included—to overthrow the Romans. Then they could finally be released from the horrible captivity they were living in, under the thumb of godless leaders who did not respect the Jews. This was the day Judas was living for. Did he betray Christ to try to bring it about sooner?

Jesus just didn't seem very interested in getting to the revolt part of the plan. It wasn't high enough on his list of priorities for Judas' taste. After all, Judas had signed up for Messiah by the sword, not miracles by the sea. Together they were supposed to defeat the Romans. Judas was into power, not poverty. He was after just rewards, not justice for the downtrodden.

Perhaps money and power played a part in Judas' decision. But ultimately, Judas betrayed Jesus *for* nothing and *because* of everything. *You just aren't what I wanted. You've never lived up to my expectations. You're going about everything all wrong.* Judas enabled the elders and the chief priests to capture Jesus because of his own profound disillusionment.

Judas couldn't let go of his idea of who the Messiah was supposed to be. In his mind he could justify many times over how Jesus had let all the Jews down by not getting them out from under Roman rule. *Maybe it was best that Jesus be removed from public life. After all, he thinks he's the Messiah.* The disillusionment in Judas' mind grew. *Yes, I'll testify to that. Yes, I'll tell you where you can find him. I'll even use a kiss to deliver him right into your hands.*

But the plan had gone awry with a question and a look. *Why?* And in the eyes of Jesus, Judas saw a heart being broken into pieces by his deceit. Jesus would only be heartbroken if he had really loved and believed in Judas all along, even as he was being betrayed. *But surely not,* Judas thought. *No man could be that loving, could he?* Unless . . . unless Jesus really was the Messiah. And then hit with the truth, Judas was undone.

Despite what we might think, the pain of the betrayer is terrible too. A false friend must live with the agony of having used a good friendship to cause harm. And the soul does not take that lightly. Whatever is gained—wealth, popularity, a new spouse—will cause hollowness on the inside. The wages of sin is death because the soul begins to die. The kiss of death was not for Jesus, though he would die; the kiss of death was for Judas.

> Then Judas, His betrayer, seeing that He had been condemned, was remorseful and brought back the thirty pieces of silver to the chief priests and elders, saying, "I have sinned by betraying innocent blood" (Matthew 27:3–4).

Remorse must have been the least of it. Agony possessed Judas as the realization of what he had done sank in. "Seeing that he had been condemned . . ." Who condemned him? His own heart. He had seen his treachery in Jesus' eyes. He had betrayed innocent blood! Perhaps he tried to explain to the religious leaders, *He is not guilty of anything! I made a mistake. He's my friend! Maybe the only real friend I've ever had.*

And they would say, "What is that to us?" *Why should we care about your friendship with this man? If he was your friend, you shouldn't have betrayed him. You were paid well for your services, Judas. Leave us.*

"Then he threw down the pieces of silver in the temple and departed." (Matthew 27:5) The sound of the silver hitting the stone echoed in the temple as the coins scattered and rolled away, reverberating inside the hollow soul of Judas as he stepped out into the night.

And back inside the temple "the chief priests took the silver pieces and said, 'It is not lawful to put them into the treasury, because they are the price of blood'" (Matthew 27:6).

Hmm, pity. Guy betrayed his friend and now has regrets, shame.

And Judas "went and hanged himself."

There was a lot of good inside Judas. Bad people don't hang themselves. A real betrayer is torn—tormented, pulled in two, double minded, and unstable. He doesn't know where to place his bet or whom to trust, so he wavers between options. He has no faith to pick a side and choose—he tries to jockey and predict, calculate and analyze—which only leads a torn heart to more anguish.

A double-minded man finds himself torn between a wife and a mistress. A double-minded woman steps on true friends to find favor with the most popular person. A double-minded broker will sell out the first offer if a better offer comes along. Betrayal never begins with the kiss; it grows in the mind long before it reaches the lips.

Judas made the worst deal ever—he should have gotten a lot more than thirty pieces of silver for a heart of pure gold. It wasn't enough. The person who betrays a friend or a spouse often finds the "reward" much smaller than they imagined, for they have shrunk their own heart in the transaction.

Judas hanged himself and never knew that his betrayal didn't kill Jesus. It was because of the world's betrayal, along with Judas', that Jesus would die. Judas couldn't grasp that this Messiah would lay down his life to set men free, to release us all from a greater oppression than Roman rule—the sin that lives in the human heart. Judas missed getting to experience this life-changing truth by just a few days—and therefore he missed knowing God's forgiveness and grace.

Judas chose to strangle the life out of his own body, believing that is what he had done in his soul.

Our greatest need in life is not the acceptance of our wrongs; it is forgiveness for them. Unfortunately, we cannot provide that kind of forgiveness for ourselves any more than we can unclog our own arteries by performing open-heart surgery on ourselves. It simply isn't possible. We can see in Judas' story what happens when we try.

Contrast his response with the response of Peter, who denied Christ three times. Peter must have felt the same feelings that Judas felt. But he came back to Jesus, because he knew love was there. He trusted that forgiveness would be available to him for the asking.

We don't know about the point in time when Jesus heard what Judas had done, but I can only imagine how much it must have increased his anguish. After all, it was why he was going to the cross. Jesus knew there would be a Judas living in all of us.

We don't know if Judas ever discovered the real value of what Christ had to offer him. It is possible that he did, as a lot can happen in the human heart in a very short period of time.

But it is also possible to believe that he died with no understanding of what Christ had come to save him from or how much he needed saving. Judas had wanted Christ to save him from the Romans, when he really needed to be saved from himself.

God's love can save us in betrayal if we will look in his eyes. It is there that we can find forgiveness for our worst treacheries. His gaze of love can melt deceit and lies, impart truth, and bring the forgiveness the human soul cannot live without.

And God's love can save the betrayed. In his embrace, we find the deepest understanding of our agony and hurt. A trusted friend turned against him, and he asked the same question we do: "Why?" He had done nothing wrong, and still he was betrayed. If God did not allow Jesus to bypass such pain, we cannot expect to fare any better. In love, he shows us personally how we can remain strong in the face of betrayal.

Some days we think we have it hard, but we don't—not while we still have the freedom to learn and grow and make better choices for the future. The hard way is never having another chance. The hard way is spending eternity looking at all we've done wrong, over and over. The hard way is choosing to live without the grace and the forgiveness that are offered to us so freely. That is the kiss of death.

Personal Reflection

This dramatic encounter between Jesus and Judas offers us a simple and life-changing lesson:

Love can forgive betrayal.

- Do you identify more with the betrayer or the betrayed? Have you been both at different times in your life? Which had more impact on you personally?

- If you have been betrayed, what is the hardest part to get past?

- If you have betrayed someone, how can you go forward with integrity and make things right? How will you deal with your guilt when it comes up repeatedly?

- Where does disappointment come from? What happens to it if it is not dealt with appropriately?

- Have you ever felt that God wasn't doing what you thought he should do? Have those feelings ever tempted you to do something you knew you shouldn't do?

- Why do you think Judas might have felt betrayed by Jesus? If Judas thought these feelings justified his actions in the beginning, why did he hang himself in the end?

Walk in the Way of Love: Be honest with yourself and God about your disappointments. Try to understand where these feelings are coming from and what is fueling them. If they are growing from unrealistic expectations, consider where you might need to take additional steps to understand where someone else is coming from and be willing to reevaluate your expectations accordingly. Guard your heart against ever thinking another's betrayal justifies your own. Whether you have betrayed someone or been betrayed, there is sufficient grace and forgiveness for you to survive it. Reaffirm your belief that the only way to change the human heart is through love—and seek to rely on God's love to bring you through your pain.

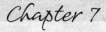

Chapter 7

A Touch of Faith

A dramatic encounter for a bleeding woman

Life-Changing Lesson:

Love floods us with peace.

Biblical Passage:

Mark 5:25–34

Now a certain woman had a flow of blood for twelve years, and had suffered many things from many physicians. She had spent all that she had and was no better, but rather grew worse. When she heard about Jesus, she came behind Him in the crowd and touched His garment. For she said, "If only I may touch His clothes, I shall be made well."

Immediately the fountain of her blood was dried up, and she felt in her body that she was healed of the affliction. And Jesus, immediately knowing in Himself that power had gone out of Him, turned around in the crowd and said, "Who touched My clothes?"

But His disciples said to Him, "You see the multitude thronging You, and You say, 'Who touched Me?'"

And He looked around to see her who had done this thing. But the woman, fearing and trembling, knowing what had happened to her, came and fell down before Him and told Him the whole truth. And He said to her, "Daughter, your faith has made you well. Go in peace, and be healed of your affliction." (Mark 5:25–34)

My name is Joan, but my husband calls me Joannie unless he's mad at me, which seems to be the norm these days. Admittedly, we're in a tough place. Brad and I have been trying to start our family for three years now. For some reason, I have been unable to get pregnant. I have a very irregular cycle and a mild case of endometriosis, but nothing so severe as to keep me from conceiving.

I find I'm easily discouraged and very drained with the whole ordeal. So I try to spend some quiet time in the mornings reading the Bible or something encouraging (no medical articles) or praying, but mostly I end up crying and then reapplying makeup before I have to get out the door for work.

I came upon her story one morning in a desperate game of Bible roulette. You know, the game where you flip through the pages and ask God to stop your finger on just the right passage for what you might need to make it through the day.

My fingers stopped on Mark 5. I skipped past the story of the demon-possessed man (clearly that was meant for my husband) and started reading at verse 25: "Now a certain woman had a flow of blood for twelve years." I had not been bleeding for twelve years, but off and on for the better part of two. My heart immediately connected with her. I had no idea what her condition might be, but I could certainly relate. A regular cycle once a month is hard enough, but when my body does its wild gymnastics at crazy times, it turns me upside down. Ask anyone who knows me. I couldn't even imagine how any woman could survive twelve years of swelling, cramping, and mood swings.

It suddenly dawned on me that if she had been bleeding for twelve years, then she would be infertile. I hate that word. I felt a flush of color rise up in my cheeks. If she was of bleeding age, then she could become pregnant, but not if her blood flow never stopped. Like me, she would be unable to conceive. Her life must have been full of the sadness and anguish of this particular pain. When you're trying to get pregnant, every time the body bleeds, so does the soul, month after painful month. She "had suffered many things from many physicians. She had spent all that she had and was no better, but rather grew worse" (Mark 5:26).

Her story was so uncomfortably familiar. It would be impossible to count all of the promises of cures that have come up empty. I thought about the discussions—okay, the fights—that Brad and I have had over money and the road ahead. What were we willing to do, and at what cost? I have already undergone several expensive treatments that only exposed the raw nerve endings of my hope to the cold air of disappointment. It was hard to blame Brad for being ready to give up, financially and emotionally.

All because of an issue of blood.

Because of an uncooperative reproductive system.

My struggle has the power to turn any hope I wake up with into a pool of disappointment. This is nothing I can control, and there is nothing I can do that I'm not already doing. There is an ache that lives inside of me that throbs like a searing, devastating hole and reminds me hourly that it is empty and angry.

I suppose every woman, and perhaps every man, has some issue of blood. Not necessarily physical bleeding like mine, but something that causes pain and threatens to drain out our very lives. When you think about it, the whole human race has messy, bloody, embarrassing problems. Issues we struggle to deal with, issues we struggle to talk about. Issues that make us bleed in ways no one else can see or understand.

A struggle with depression

A child who has lost his or her way and makes devastating choices

An eating disorder

An addiction

"When she heard about Jesus, she came up behind him in the crowd and touched his garment. For she said, 'If only I may touch his clothes, I shall be made well.'"

It's obvious that she was a planner, a woman of action, and that she talked to herself, just like I do. She decided what she would do, and she made her plan accordingly. Maybe she turned it over in her mind a few times, debating, you know, like women do. Maybe, like me in many of my plans, she went from thinking, *What good would it do?* to wondering what she had to lose by trying. But the truth was, she could lose a lot, because she was unclean by Jewish law. Leviticus 15:25–28 is pretty clear on the matter:

> *If a woman has a discharge of blood for many days, other than at the time of her customary impurity, she shall be unclean. Every bed that she lies on shall be unclean. Everything that she sits on shall be unclean. Whoever touches those things shall be unclean . . . But if she is cleansed of her discharge,*

then she shall count for herself seven days, and after that she shall be clean. And on the eighth day she shall take for herself two turtledoves or two young pigeons and bring them to the priest as a sacrifice. And the priest shall make atonement for her before the Lord.

I had previously wondered why this woman didn't just walk right up to Jesus and ask him to heal her as others had already done. But after reading this passage, it is clear. According to the law, she was unclean and had been for twelve years. And not only was Jesus a good Jew, but many thought him holier than most of the religious leaders. It was impossible for her to believe that he would ever come near her, let alone lay his hands on her and touch her.

And I guess in my heart of hearts, I wondered if Jesus would touch me. Infertility can make a woman feel not only sad and lonely, but defective and inferior. I don't even fully know why. In my head I knew it was wrong to feel that way, but I did sometimes. Some of it could have been my imagination, but there were times I choked back the tears and told someone I was struggling with infertility, and my confession was met with anything but support. I remember one friend who physically moved back a little in her chair—almost like she recoiled. She mumbled something about feeling sorry for me, which is the worst, and then—this could be where I imagined it—she pulled her daughter right up close to her side. I'm sure she wasn't even aware she did it. I wished I hadn't been aware of it either.

Twelve years of pain and desperation combined with desperate hope fueled this dramatic encounter with Jesus of Nazareth. In the middle of a dusty road, on an unknown date in history, time stood still and her life would be forever altered. Because of her fear that he would never touch her, she realized her only chance would be to touch him. But if she were caught, she would be cut off from her people, or even stoned to death, for what she did. But what did she have to lose?

The woman moved into the crowd, careful not to touch anyone, trying not to be close enough to be accidentally touched by them. How could she touch Jesus without being noticed? Then she thought, *I don't have to touch him. If I just touch his clothes, or any part of his garment, that will be enough.* And her faith was born. She opened her heart as she opened her hand.

But why did she touch the hem of his garment? She must have been on the ground. The hem, or the fringe at the bottom of Jesus' garment, was made up of tassels. Numbers 15:38–41 says, "Speak to the children of Israel: Tell them to make tassels on the corners of their garments throughout their generations, and to put a blue thread in the tassels of the corners. And you shall have the tassel, that you may look upon it and remember all the commandments of the LORD and do them . . . I am the LORD your God."

Wearing the tassel represented a desire to remember and follow all the commandments of the Lord, including a commandment she was intentionally breaking. That tassel is what she touched. There was Jesus, wearing a tassel honoring the law of God, yet walking through the dirt and dust of everyday life. And there was the woman, on the ground, in the dirt, torn between the law (this is what I know) and the pain (this is where I live). She probably wanted to yank the tassel off his garment and rip it to shreds. How I could relate to her!

Such a desperate plight. She must have thought, *Is there more than this law that leaves me feeling hopeless and filthy? Please, can you help me?* And that touch was her bold assertion of the answer—*I believe you can. I am trusting that there is more to this life than this issue of blood that makes me unclean. I believe it is* you. *You can make me clean.* She didn't even know the full extent of her belief.

But Jesus did, and he stopped for her. And, indeed, he still stops for us.

He turns around and asks, "Who touched me?"

I love what happens with the disciples here. They don't know the answer and they get all flustered and defensive. "You see the multitude thronging you and you say, 'Who touched me?'" In today's language, "Come on, you've got to be kidding. Look at all these people. [Nudging each other] He wants to know who touched him. James? Did you touch him? Okay, well, that narrows it down to about seventy-five prospects then . . ."

But Jesus wasn't asking the disciples. Jesus wasn't even asking the crowd. Jesus was asking her. He had been truly touched by her, because she had touching faith—the kind of faith that reaches out with the hunger to touch more than this world has to offer. And he never passes that by.

I'll bet he never even looked at her. This is the kind of dignity that he offers to those of us with bleeding pain. He saw her, even though the disciples didn't. The crowd had no idea. She might have even gotten away with it in the eyes of everyone else. But wasn't he really asking her, "Who touched you?" She knew he saw her.

He was giving her a chance to tell her story. *Step out of the crowd; don't hide or run away.*

Oh, she must have been afraid. *What will happen if I confess? Do I tell them that I am healed? Have I made him unclean? Will I be stoned for this?*

Trembling, she fell down before him and told her story....

The account in Scripture does not tell us what she said. No doubt because mere words could never quite capture what she must have felt in that moment and how she poured her heart out at his feet. But perhaps the absence of her words leaves you and me room to insert our own.

And a few days later after my game of Bible roulette, that's exactly what I did. I knelt before him and wept through my story, telling him the whole truth. I reached out and touched the hem of his garment. And when I was finished I read the words of God saying to me exactly what he said to her that day: "Daughter, your faith has made you well. Go in peace."

Peace. Quiet. Still inside. No more angst and churning. It is this peace that love brings to our issues of blood, a powerful security that brings deep serenity. Love will touch you when you are unclean.

We don't use the word *unclean* anymore, but we still know in our souls exactly what it means. This is why being free of drugs and alcohol is called being *clean*. Telling the truth after you have lied is called *coming clean*. To be cleared of wrong and blame is to have a *clean* record. And more personally, letting go of bitterness and resentment toward God, for life not going the way you thought it should, is cleansing beyond measure. Loved, forgiven, washed, pure, clean. "Go in peace."

I have wondered so many times what happened to her. Was she received back into her community as a clean woman? Did she eventually conceive a child? The story never goes any further. But she was washed clean by love, and she went forward in peace. There is not much more that any woman could want, myself included.

Peace is ours when we reach to touch love and find instead that love has touched us. And in that touch the storm is calmed and the bleeding is stopped.

Remember the ending instructions of the law from Leviticus? How the woman was to wait seven days and then take two turtledoves to the priest as an offering? Jesus didn't tell her to go to the priest. He didn't tell her to bring an offering. She didn't need to—she had already seen the Priest, and soon a different sacrifice would be made, once and for all.

Her touch did make him unclean, yet he took that uncleanness upon himself. Her bleeding had stopped, and his had not yet begun. But it soon would, and one day she would hear someone say that he offered his blood to wash away the sin of the world. And because of her issue of blood, she would understand this on a level deep inside her soul. And she would continue to tell her story to anyone who would listen, every chance she had.

Personal Reflection

This dramatic encounter between Jesus and a bleeding woman offers us a simple and life-changing lesson:

Love floods us with peace.

- In your mind, what constitutes an "issue of blood"?

- Is there still shame associated with sickness, such as HIV, or other issues of blood?

- Think of a person in your life dealing with an issue of blood who might need some deep encouragement. What can you do to help?

- Have you ever felt torn between God's law and the desire of your heart? How did you handle it?

- Can you be honest with anyone close to you about an issue of blood that you might have?

Walk in the Way of Love: We don't have to suffer in silence. Reach out for God's love—not just for immediate comfort, but for the kind of touch he gave to the woman with the issue of blood. Put your whole heart into reaching for what you most desire on the inside: a love that will touch you in your messy state and bring deep security. It is possible to discover what Joannie did: when you reach for the love of God, you will find that it has been reaching for you longer than you could know.

Epilogue

Taking a Walk
in the Wheat Field

*S*ometimes a dramatic encounter isn't revealed until after it has occurred.

You might have even been there when it took place, but the meaning or the message just didn't make sense until later. Because life has a way of presenting challenges we can't figure out, challenges that send us riffling through our resources trying to make sense of things. You might recall an event in your life when the meaning or the message didn't "click" until long after the event had happened.

I think this is what must have happened with Peter and many of the disciples as they lived out the days and months and years following the horrible death of their friend and leader. I identify so deeply with Peter in the way he constantly struggled to understand Jesus when he walked the earth and even more so after it was over on earth. In studying each of these dramatic encounters, I could almost feel his strong presence next to Jesus as he stood beside him to face the Gadarene demoniac, or at other times, like in the Garden of Gethsemane when his own anger and emotion overtook him. But of all the things that could be said about Peter, he was a man who struggled hard with faith. He wanted to understand everything and he wanted what he heard to make sense. Perhaps he felt a little thick at times, like he had to run to catch up to the others, but run he did. Sometimes he didn't stop until he passed them. And then he might sit down to think some more.

So I thought this last story would be a fitting epilogue to the seven dramatic encounters, because the lesson of the encounter landed much later, as it often does for us. After Jesus was gone, the disciples had to keep going back over the things Jesus had said and done. They had to think about what it meant for their lives and how they were supposed to translate that into what they were supposed to do and how they were supposed to live. It was a lot for Peter to process, and it probably frustrated him that the understanding came bit by bit, not all at one time.

Another parable He put forth to them, saying: "The kingdom of heaven is like a man who sowed good seed in his field; but while men slept, his enemy came and sowed tares among the wheat and went his way. But when the grain had sprouted and produced a crop, then the tares also appeared. So the servants of the owner came and said to him, "Sir, did you not sow good seed in your field? How then does it have tares?" He said to them, "An enemy has done this." The servants said to him, "Do you want us then to go and gather them up?" But he said, "No, lest while you gather up the tares you also uproot the wheat with them. Let both grow together until the harvest, and at the time of harvest I will say to the reapers, "First gather together the tares and bind them in bundles to burn them, but gather the wheat into my barn." (Matthew 13:24–30)

Jesus was gone. For Peter, his death was finally sinking in. After the horrific events of that evening, which were still hard to think about, they'd all had that amazing and mysterious time on the beach together. Peter had seen him on the shore, and they all practically drowned trying to get to him fast enough. None of them could believe he was there and cooking fish! But since that glorious breakfast, there had been nothing. No other sign, no word, just the settled emptiness of his absence.

Not that Peter had forgotten any of Jesus' words—they were reverberating inside him, but it was hard for the big man to know what to do with it all. That's probably why he was standing in the middle of a wheat field in the middle of the night. Somehow it reminded him of his Lord, and he could think about things.

Like the time he told them a parable about this wheat field. They had crossed it the day before, and later when Jesus was teaching, he'd brought it up. In fact, he used a lot of the things they all experienced together in his teaching with people. Many of these examples were new to Peter. After all, he was a fisherman, not a farmer, so he didn't always "get it." But that never seemed to bother Jesus.

This particular parable, though, really stuck with Peter and most of the other men. In fact, the day Jesus told it, no one could really understand what it meant. But no one wanted to ask in front of everyone else, so after all the crowds had gone for the day and they were finally relaxing in the evening, one of the men, Peter thought it might have been John, actually came right out and asked Jesus, "Explain to us the parable of the tares of the field."

So Jesus said to them, "He who sows the good seed is

the Son of Man. The field is the world, the good seeds are the sons of the kingdom, but the tares are the sons of the wicked one. The enemy who sowed them is the devil, the harvest is the end of the age, and the reapers are the angels. Therefore as the tares are gathered and burned in the fire, so it will be at the end of this age. The Son of Man will send out His angels, and they will gather out of His kingdom all things that offend, and those who practice lawlessness, and will cast them into the furnace of fire. There will be wailing and gnashing of teeth. Then the righteous will shine forth as the sun in the kingdom of their Father.

"He who has ears to hear, let him hear!" (Matthew 13:37–43).

Honestly? No one liked it when he said that. Because if for some reason, they hadn't gotten it by then, they knew they had missed it. But what Peter had come to understand was that he might not miss it forever. He had lost count of how many of Jesus' stories had gone over his head initially only to end up weeks later living deep inside his heart. It was like the stories were on a time delay and days later something would happen and a light would come on. This parable of the wheat and the tares was one such example.

But it also made him very sad. He wanted to see Jesus coming toward him in this field, talking as he walked. Much as he did for so many of the days they were together. Explaining things, teaching them, helping them make sense of the world. Battling for truth with those pious religious people and show-ing them a side of humanity (and divinity) that none of them had ever seen or heard of before or since.

Peter began to speak out loud in the field. More accu-rately, he began to pray, but he would not have called it that at the time. "It's hard to understand all this, you know." Just hearing his voice in the moonlight talking to Jesus brought a lump to his throat. "I wish you were still here to help me fig-ure this out." He paused. "I came here because of that story you told about the wheat and the tares. Remember when John asked you to explain it to us? I wanted to ask, too, and I didn't want you to think I didn't understand it, but I didn't." He put his head down. "But you probably knew that.

"I think I get it now. I mean, not fully, but more than I did when I first heard you tell it. I mean, I cut off that soldier's ear, and I said I didn't know you—I know we got that square, but

I was thinking about how much I might have looked like one of these tares in those moments. And how, if somebody was looking at me from the outside, they might not think I was one of the good ones, you know, the wheat. They might think I was just some wild rye grass that the enemy had planted. But I know . . ." He choked up and could hardly get the words out. "I know you know I'm not.

"I guess all I'm saying is that a lot of things you said are finally sinking in. I thought you might want to know that." He paused. "And that I really miss you around here. It's just not the same."

Peter walked out of the wheat field in the moonlight and headed back toward town.

Just like Peter, I grapple with the complexity of life. There are so many things that seem well beyond my scope of understanding:

Why is there so much suffering in the world?
Why do evil people seem to prosper?
Is God responsible for everything?

When I come face-to-face with many of my own questions

and wonderings, it prompts me to metaphorically "take a walk in the wheat field"—to stand in the moonlight with my prayers and questions and try to sort things out. And I have come back to this story of the wheat and the tares more times than I can count.

I am a sorter from a long line of sorters. I am "category" driven, and that is a gift as well as a problem. I like to know where to put things. I love order. I want my kitchen and my closet to be nice and tidy, and without fully thinking it through, I can begin to expect life to cooperate in the same way—like relationships are just pairs of shoes to be lined up or that problems can just be pressed and hung up in color-coded order. But truthfully, I feel more comfortable that way because life is messy and often can be scary.

Our love or even need for order is right and good and normal, if properly understood, but the reason this story is a dramatic encounter for me is because there are clearly things that will never fit into simplistic categories and should never be forced to. We live with complex situations that often refuse to fit into nice, neat categories. It was a lesson that Jesus felt was worth the time it would take to teach it. It remains a lesson that keeps me walking in the wheat fields today, when I sense God saying . . .

Careful, Nicole . . .

Not so fast. Look at it again, Nicole.

Aren't you missing something?

What do you think I see when I look at this?

Without the Spirit guiding me, I could make a royal mess of the wheat field. I could easily pull out all the wheat and have a plot choked with tares in my desire to tidy up the kingdom. But God runs a different organization—the kind that leaves the ninety-nine sheep to go and look for the one, the kind that would let tares grow up right along the wheat so as not to lose even one stalk of the good stuff.

It does make me feel a little better that in the story the servants of the owner were just like me. "Do you want us to go and gather them up?" they asked him. "C'mon, Lord—we can have this field in tip-top shape in no time at all. I know the enemy did this, but give us a little time and we can reclaim it!" We could get out there and get everything divided into nice, neat stacks:

The good and the bad
The pretty and the ugly

The saved and the lost

The useful and the useless

And very clearly, without any ambiguity, the owner, God, says a resounding, "No. You don't know what you're doing. Rather than helping, you might actually make it worse."

"Oh."

Isn't it just like God to be unwilling to lose even one stalk of wheat? Isn't it just like us to be willing to lose as many as necessary to have the field looking better? But for someone to hurt one little stalk of wheat (especially one that might look like a tare) is simply not worth the risk to God. Leave the tares alone. *Don't pull up anything,* he says. *It's not your job. You don't know, you can't tell, and should you make a mistake, something very important might be lost.*

The plant in question here, the tare, most scholars believe to be the bearded darnel or rye grass that flourishes in countries along the Mediterranean Sea. It resembles wheat so closely that it can prosper in the cornfields and be almost indistinguishable until fully grown. The inner coats of these seeds often harbor seriously poisonous fungus growths that, if eaten by humans or animals, will cause dizziness and vomiting and sometimes even death. (See *All the Plants of the Bible* by Winifred Walker.)

Consider if accidentally you hurt the wheat and kept the tares alive because their outside appearance made them undistinguishable from each other. What if the very real evil that grows in the world would be multiplied if you made it your mission to rid the field of the tares? You could end up doing the exact opposite of what you set out to accomplish. "No," God says, "the cost is too high. You might not recognize the good stuff, so leave it all alone. As hard as it is, and will be, you have to live with the tares." We must take our hands off the harvesting and do the other jobs He gave us to do.

But the temptation to sort the wheat is almost irresistible. One of the very best reasons that people give for not following Christ is Christians. People outside the faith see Christians as "too sure" of everything. They live arrogantly because all of their problems, if they admit to having any, fit in nice, tidy compartments or categories, like "sinful" and "holy."

I suppose that's fair, but I can argue with equal fervor that even though that may be what some Christians do, that is not what Christ taught us to do. He taught us to live in this complex world with discernment but also with an internal resolution to resist overly simplistic categories. And it's hard to demonstrate this truth when many Christians remain so unconvinced of it.

But all it takes is one humble believer—not an "open wide, shove it down your throat" person—one genuine person of faith who follows Christ's way of refusing to put life's issues into simplistic categories. And the argument against faith just melts away.

Lord, make me willing to live in the complexity of uncertainty with my surety in other things, like your love. Convince me that there could be more damage done by unknowingly hurting one good stalk of wheat than by leaving the weeds to grow alongside. I am sure that of the wheat and the tares in this field, you know very clearly which is which. Not only is it not my job to determine this—I think it's possible you would withhold this clarity to keep us from judging others. I know you too well and trust you too much to ever want to be in the way of what you are doing in this world.

Acknowledgments

$\mathcal{W}$hile I am fully, and sometimes painfully, aware of my limitations, you, dear reader, may not be. You may not know just how many people have helped me in order to allow you to hold this finished work in your hands. You may not know that much like raising a child, it takes a village to produce a book. I'd like to introduce you to my village.

Amy Cella and all of team Fresh Brewed Life—you are gifts from the Giver of the best gifts. To work with you and have you in my life—Michelle Randall, David and Leah Simmons, Christina Smith, Barbara Smith, Kate Huffman, and Pat Anzures—You make it possible for me to write and I'm grateful.

Medora Heilbron—your vision and leadership have made an enormous difference in my company and in my life. Besides adding Yiddish into my vocabulary, you have brought tremendous joy to my heart.

Mom and David—you are such a wonderful part of team FBL and our lives. Your encouragement and support is as unending as the shoreline—any writer would be blessed to have you as parents.

Dad and Ellen—your faithful calls and prayers, as well as your interest, were such a help along the way, and I'm grateful to finally have something to show you.

Carolyn Denny—thank you for your grace, manifested in extensions and patience in biblical proportions. Your encouragement really helped me through some tough spots. Whoever first saw your genius deserves a lot of praise—they and you have my gratitude.

Vanessa Hollis—thank you for your sisterly encouragement and prayers and for reminding me of the importance of finishing this book—if for no one else but myself.

Mel Berger—it was a privilege to have you as my agent on this book—and while I can't say yet that I'm looking forward to the next one, I'm grateful for your help on this one.

Chuck Swindoll—thank you for the inspiration and insight that you brought to our group in Israel and that you continue to bring sometimes weekly via CDs and tapes. You have no idea how many lives you are touching all over the world.

My friends and sisters at Women of Faith—Mary, Luci, Marilyn, Patsy, Thelma, and Sheila—you've blessed my life in countless ways. But this year, thank you for the freedom to cut back my calendar to pursue my dreams. You are in my heart always.

And to my family and friends who have supported me and forgiven me for not being at this particular party or on that particular trip. I'm thankful for each of you who has graciously accepted these words from me: "I wish I could, but I have to write." I couldn't have gotten here without that kind of support.

And to my husband, Roy—you add so much joy to my life, and you strengthen me inside with your love and emotional support, which I've needed so much throughout this long process. May God give you back tenfold all that you sacrificed along the way to help me as I wrote each page.

And to the God of heaven—for my own dramatic encounter with you, I will be eternally grateful.